FROM HEAD TO HEART

D1456487

LAURIE
CLARK
Liberty Church

FROM

HEAD

TO

HEART

ROBERT S. MCGEE
AND RUJON MORRISON

SERVANT PUBLICATIONS
ANN ARBOR, MICHIGAN

Vine Books is an imprint of Servant Publications especially designed to serve
evangelical Christians.

Published by Servant Publications
P.O. Box 8617
Ann Arbor, Michigan 48107

Cover design: PAZ Design Group, Salem, Oregon

97 98 99 00 10 9 8 7 6 5 4 3 2 1

Printed in the United States of America
ISBN 0-89283-952-X

LIBRARY OF CONGRESS CATALOGING-IN-PUBLICATION DATA

McGee, Robert S.
From head to heart / Robert S. McGee and Rujon Morrison.
    p. cm.
ISBN 0-89283-952-X
1. Faith. 2. Trust in God—Christianity. I. Morrison Rujon. II. Title.
BV4637. M38   1997
234—dc21   96-48995
                                                    CIP

CONTENTS

ONE

THE JOURNEY FROM HEAD TO HEART

It was 2:00 A.M. and I (Robert) was still tossing and turning in my bed. My mind raced, and nothing I tried would quiet it. I had big plans in the making, important plans, but they were not working out. Key people were not cooperating. Overcome by anxiety and anger, my spirit cried out, *How can this be happening? How can my well-laid plans be going so wrong?*

A torrent of I-shoulds flooded my mind with self-condemnation: *I should have made better decisions. I should be able to handle the situation. I should be able to trust God and be at perfect peace.* Why couldn't what I knew about God in my head comfort my heart? Why, in spite of everything I had experienced in the past, in spite of all the proofs of his blessings and his faithfulness, why did I still feel so totally overwhelmed?

In times past, God had often met me in the midst of my difficulties. Looking back, I could clearly see how his loving hand had led me through each of those situations, and how he had allowed me to learn and mature because of them. So what was wrong now? If I were to invite God into my current struggle, he would be right there beside me. He would give me the strength I needed, and he would bring me through in peace. I knew that was true. So why couldn't I do it?

With great effort, I concentrated on pulling my attention off my problems and focusing it onto God. I asked him to show me why I was having such a hard time trusting him with this situation.

And then it all came back to me.

Many years ago, a man filed a law suit against me over a minor dispute. An extremely wealthy businessman, he had a history of instigating this type of conflict, then drawing it out in court as long as possible. He seemed to thoroughly enjoy the agony and frustration he caused others. I tried and tried to settle the disagreement in a fair and peaceable manner, but he steadfastly refused to cooperate. For four years I struggled to resolve the matter, but each attempt was met with hostility. Finally we ended up in court. And wouldn't you know, the trial was set for a week during which I was scheduled to speak at a large convention in Florida.

"Can't you get the court date postponed?" I asked my attorney. "I agreed to this speaking engagement over a year ago. If I back out now, it will really leave them in a lurch."

"The date can't be postponed," the attorney said, "but don't worry about it. This is such a trivial matter that you don't even need to be there."

So, taking the attorney's advice, I went on to Florida. I would leave the matter in God's hands. He would deal with this person who had unjustly tormented my life for so long.

After my presentation, I called my secretary to see whether or not the case had been heard, and if so, what had happened. As soon as she said, "Hello," I knew something was wrong.

"The court did try the case," she told me hesitantly, "and it was determined that the man should not be awarded damages."

"Sounds great," I said. "So what's the problem?"

The problem was that the man had successfully presented himself as a helpless victim in the case, and the judge had ordered me to pay all his attorney's costs. Since the matter had been dragging on so long, those fees had really added up.

"How much?" I asked.

"Ninety thousand dollars."

Ninety thousand dollars? I was so stunned I couldn't say a word. I mumbled something, then hung up the telephone and sank into a nearby chair. I was absolutely overwhelmed. It wasn't just the injustice of it all, nor even the huge debt that now hung over my head. The worst thing was that I felt that God had betrayed me. I had missed that court date because I was faithfully serving him. I had *trusted* him and look what had happened!

"Why, God?" my heart demanded. "Why are you letting this happen to me? Why...." I stopped in mid-sentence. "...You have no right to question God!" I scolded myself. "How dare you challenge his wisdom?" I struggled to keep from believing what my mind was insisting was so—that God had let me down.

But that had been years ago. I had matured a great deal

since then. Now here were those same old emotions flooding over me again, and with an intensity that astonished me.

Here in my bed, in the wee hours of the morning, I had prayed, "Dear God, show me why I can't trust you as I ought." God answered my prayer by showing me exactly when and where it was that I had erected a barrier between my head knowledge about the faithful trustworthiness of God, and my heart's acceptance of the truth I knew.

The painful memory of that event, and my resulting disappointment and disillusionment with God, acted as a magnet that pulled back other memories of times when I had been disappointed and disillusioned. My head insisted, "God is faithful and trustworthy." Yet my heart cried out, "I can't count on God! He will let me down." That night in my bed God showed me that I had allowed a wall of distrust to build up and block from my heart the peace I so desperately sought.

For all these years, that barrier had been building inside of me. I had no idea it was there, but God knew. He also knew that unless it was exposed and destroyed, I could never know the peace that passes understanding.

A Common Problem

I know this head-to-heart blockage is not unique to me. Time and time again I have heard Christians say, "I know all about justification (or holiness or grace or forgiveness or obedience or regeneration or peace). I can give you a definition of it. I can even back up my definition with Scripture.

But I just can't seem truly to *own* it. It is just not real to me."

A friend once told me that the few inches between his head and his heart were the most mysterious and stubborn distance he had ever encountered. He said, "No matter how hard I try, I just can't make what I know to be God's truth travel down that short space and touch my heart."

I know exactly what he means, and I'm sure you do too. We all have stubborn barriers that block that short distance.

Head Knowledge Versus Heart Knowledge

The problem is, there is a big difference between *head knowledge* and *heart knowledge*. Head knowledge is what we know about something on an intellectual basis. It is the definition of something. It's the facts and dates and statistics that tell us about it. It can include an understanding of how a thing works, perhaps what it does and why. Head knowledge is a wonderful thing. We read and study and go to school to get it. But there is a big limitation to head knowledge; it can be distorted by many things—our own experiences and the experiences of others, the teachings to which we have been exposed, examples set by other people. This type of knowledge is humanly-initiated, humanly-inspired, and humanly-limited. It gives us the *illusion* of truth and understanding. But that is all it is—an illusion.

Heart knowledge, on the other hand, relates to a type of understanding that is practical and applicable. Going a step further, heart knowledge actually makes room for revelation from God. When true, it is God-initiated, God-inspired, and God-illuminated. Heart knowledge allows us to grasp onto truth with a comprehension that reaches to the very core of our beings. It is knowledge that is integrated into us, and actually becomes a part of us.

Why are there such persistent and formidable barriers between our heads and our hearts? How can we identify the barriers within ourselves? And, most important of all, how can we break those barriers down and clear the way so that what we know about God can move on into our hearts?

Excellent questions. It just so happens that they are the very ones we will be considering in this book. And the answers will bring us much more than mere head knowledge. If we allow them to, those answers will show us how we can know God in the way he intended—fully and with our innermost spirits.

Barriers to Heart Knowledge

So often people cry out, "If only God would reveal himself to me!"

Well, God *has* revealed himself to us. Everything we need to know is right there in the pages of his Holy Word, the Bible. We know, for instance, that God is *holy.* We know he grants us his *grace.* We know he *justifies* us and *forgives* us when we *sin* against him. We know he requires *obedience* from us, and that he offers us *regeneration.* And we know that he affords us a wonderful and eternal *peace* that passes all understanding.

The question is not, "Why won't God reveal himself?" but "Why isn't God's revelation making a difference in my life?"

The Big Five

In the chapters that follow, we will be considering five barriers that frequently bar the way between head and heart:

1. *Language barriers:* These barriers are caused by the limitations of language. They inhibit our ability to express concepts in words. We know the words. We can say them, but they stay in our heads and do not change our hearts.

2. *Experience barriers:* These barriers arise out of the painful experiences of our lives. Because of their negative nature, they adversely affect our view of God and our understanding of the dynamics of our relationship with him.

3. *Distorted belief barriers:* These barriers arise from erroneous, misunderstood, or misguided teachingsthat lead us to distorted beliefs.

4. *Emotional defense barriers:* These are the barriers we design and erect in an attempt to protect ourselves from being hurt by others—including God.

5. *Control barriers:* These are the barriers we put in place in an effort to stay in control of our lives. They are our way of saying, "No, I will not completely yield myself to my relationship with God and his authority! I will do it my way!"

Because we need more than the above definitions of these barriers, we have written this book. As you turn the following pages, it is our hope that you will not merely be amassing more head-knowledge. We want to help you personalize what you read.

How do these barriers affect you specifically? We will be considering them in relation to eight words which are pivotal to our grasp of the nature of God and his work in our lives. We have used these words above as we described what God has revealed about himself in Scripture. They are:

Holy

Grace

Justification

Sin

Forgiveness

Obedience

Regeneration

Peace

These simple words are not very helpful in this format. Come explore with us through the next several chapters as we discuss these words in relation to the five barriers. It may be that you will see yourself in one of the examples. You may be reading someone's else's story and suddenly exclaim, "That's me! That's my barrier, too!"

Then again, you may not.

Either way, it is our prayer that in your reading of this book, something even more significant than spotting your particular barriers will happen: you will become sensitive to whatever it is that is keeping you from the life God wants you to experience. It is our further prayer that as you become more sensitive, you will learn to rely on him to lead you to break down your own barriers.

A Suggestion

To help you make the information you will be reading in the chapters become more specifically applicable to your own life, we have prepared a series of short evaluations. These are located in the appendix at the end of the book. Before you go any further, we would like to suggest that you turn to that section and take a few minutes to test yourself. You may be surprised to see the degree to which the barriers in your life are keeping you from experiencing the reality of God.

Then, with your own personal evaluation in hand, you will be ready to look at the foundational barrier upon which all other barriers are built: the language barrier.

Questions for Reflection and Discussion

1. Can you think of an experience like Robert's—one where you knew God's truth in your head, but had a contradictory message in your heart? How did you deal with this?

2. Try to identify other thoughts that you know are "head knowledge" versus contradictory "heart thoughts." Are these at odds with one another? Does it seem that they

"war" against one another? How does 2 Corinthians 10: 3-6 challenge us in this battle?

3. Why must God "initiate, inspire, and illuminate" his truth in order for us to have a heart experience? How do we participate in this process?

4. Look at the definition for each of the barriers. Try to think of personal examples of each of these: a thought, a belief, a rule, a vow, or a message you have received which would fit into each category. How have these affected the way you view yourself? How have they affected the way you relate to others and to God?

TWO

BARRIER #1:
LANGUAGE

"When I picture heaven," Kate says, "I picture a place of wonderful splendor, a majestic realm with crystal lakes and a golden highway lined with glorious white mansions. The entrance gate is formed of one huge pearl, and beside that gate an enormous, vicious bulldog stands guard."

A *bulldog?*

Yep, a bulldog. "I grew up hearing Martin Luther's great hymn, *A Mighty Fortress Is Our God*," Kate explains, "and soon I was singing right along with the adults: *A mighty fortress is our God, a bulldog never failing!*"

Language is a funny thing. If the words don't fit in with our frame of reference, we simply adjust the words to something we can understand. Then we transfer that concept into a picture which settles firmly in our minds. Once the picture is rooted there, it is extremely difficult to change it. Does Kate know there is no bulldog guarding the gates of heaven? Of course she does. But that bulldog picture remains a persistent part of her perception of heaven.

Not long ago I read *The Gift of Dyslexia*, by Ronald P.

Davis[1]. Davis tells about discovering that his dyslexia worsened while he was sculpting. *Why would this be?* he wondered. As he thought about it, he realized that when he was creating a sculpture, he was using his mind differently than when he was trying to read. After months of trial and error, and after a great deal of experimentation, he discovered how he could keep his mind oriented in such a way that he could finally begin to read.

Certain common words continued to disorient him, however, simple words such as *and, but, as, there, if.* What was the common factor in those words? The answer: none of them had a visual counterpart. Davis couldn't *see* those words. This realization gave him an idea. He set to work making clay models to represent each of these words, and then, using those clay models, he created an entire scene for each one. From then on when he encountered those words, his mind was able to recall something visual. Now he could "see" the words.

Since my children and I are all dyslexic, this was an amazing discovery to me. It made so much sense. As we went through a similar process of making abstract words visible, it occurred to me that many of the important words of our Christian faith have no concrete visual counterpart. Could this be the first step in understanding why so many of us have trouble moving Christian concepts from our heads down to our hearts?

THE FIRST HURDLE

When we were children, we learned to speak by a simple process: someone showed us an object and said the name for it, and we tried to repeat the word. This was repeated over and over again until we knew the word. This *see, hear, touch* method of learning generally worked well. But now that we are well beyond the see-the-pretty-yellow-flower and pat-the-nice-kitty stage, there is a problem. Many words are abstract; there are no concrete pictures to attach to them. They refer to things that can't be seen, heard, smelled, tasted, or felt. This is especially true of theological words.

That's not to say we aren't able to understand ideas that can't be seen or touched. We certainly can. One way is to relate an unknown word or concept to something we already know. For example, I read about a man who was born blind. His little son was telling him about the toy fire truck he got for his birthday: "Its wheels move, the ladders go up and down, and it's bright red." Then the little boy paused thoughtfully and asked, "Daddy? Do you even know what red looks like?"

"Sure," his dad said. "It looks hot, just the way fire feels."

He was right. Comparison is a good approach if something comparable is available. But what if there isn't anything comparable? What if you are dealing with something or someone totally unique? What if it is God himself you are trying to understand?

In our attempt to understand a force and power as

beyond our comprehension as God is, we develop words and labels to describe his characteristics and attributes. Then we create definitions for these words and labels. Unfortunately, what tends to happen is that we end up with a dictionary in our heads—and a void in our hearts.

In our effort to find comparisons for our incomparable God, we try to pull him down to where he is something more simple and concrete, something we can understand. For instance, a common description of the Holy Trinity is that they are like water, vapor, and ice; they are three different manifestations of the same thing. Ah, but what an inadequately simplistic comparison! Although our intentions are good, our efforts leave us with a severely distorted image of God's true character and his incomprehensible attributes.

WHERE DOES IT LEAVE US?

Teresa and Howard were so proud of their little daughter, Amanda. According to them, she was the cutest, the smartest, the most talented baby ever to grace the earth. Although it meant cutting way back on their standard of living, Teresa and Howard agreed on work schedules that would allow one or the other of them always to be at home with their daughter. They wanted to raise Amanda themselves, to watch over her and be a constant part of her life. From her earliest months, they wanted to teach her about God.

Two weeks after Amanda's second birthday, while Teresa was washing up the lunch dishes, Amanda climbed out of her bed and slipped outside to ride her new tricycle. Never will Teresa be able to forget the horror of the next few minutes—the screech of brakes, her neighbor's hysterical screams, the shriek of the ambulance siren. Little Amanda did not survive the night.

"Why, why, why?" Teresa demanded over and over again. "We are good people, godly people. We cared so much about our child. We did everything right. How could God have taken our baby away?"

None of us could possibly blame Teresa and Howard for grieving the loss of their baby. Yet they will never be able to find peace again until they escape the terribly destructive process in which they are now caught. They have ceased *trying to know* God and have started *trying to understand* him. The difference is critical.

Coming to know God is absolutely essential. He reveals his loving nature to us in so many ways. We see his faithfulness even when we are not responding faithfully to him. We experience his power in our lives in ways we can neither foresee nor imagine. As we experience God's creation, we are overwhelmed by his great power.

And then something happens that shakes us to the very core of our being. Instead of remembering who God is and all his qualities we have experienced in the past, we struggle frantically trying to understand it all intellectually. *How can these characteristics possibly* all *be true?* we demand. *How can God be loving and in control, yet still let this thing happen?* We are desperate to understand because we believe that will allow us to feel more in control.

Because we never can understand intellectually, it is right here that we leave behind our openness to *know* God in a deeper, fuller way. The simple fact is, he is God and we are human. His ways are infinitely higher than our ways. When we depend on our own reasoning, we only find ourselves more desperate and more frustrated. The end result is a penetrating sense of alienation.

When we strive to define God on our own terms, our efforts to understand him supersede our efforts to develop a relationship with him. Therefore, instead of taking comfort in his infinite love, instead of resting in the peace of his ultimate wisdom, we are driven to try to understand why he allows specific events to enter our lives.

"Why, God?" we cry out in our pain. "How could you let this happen?"

Since we cannot understand what is happening, we conclude that either God isn't able to control the situation, or else that he just doesn't care. In our attempts to make rational sense of something our minds cannot understand, we end up in turmoil. The peace of God becomes nothing but an empty platitude.

This, then, is where our heart barriers begin—with the limitations of our language. Let's use our eight words to see how this barrier obstructs our ability to experience God's truth.

Holy

The French atheist Voltaire once said, "The Bible says 'God made man in his own image,' and now man has returned the favor." Voltaire wasn't far off the mark. We are guilty of having made God man-sized by saddling him with a type of holiness we can understand. This has created a huge problem: If we see God as nothing more than a super-person, how can we ever fully trust him? When tragedy strikes, as it did Teresa and Howard, we are left with nothing but an anguished cry of "Why?" In response, God asks his own questions

To whom will you compare me?
Or who is my equal? says the Holy One.   ISAIAH 40:25

God is holy. We know this because the Scriptures declare it hundreds of times over. We know that it is God's holiness that makes him who he is, and that dictates his constancy. In Hebrews 13:8, we read that "Jesus Christ is the same yesterday and today and forever." James 1:17 describes him as a Father "who does not change like shifting shadows." Forever and ever, from before the dawn of history throughout endless eternity, God is sure and unfailing.

Typically, we think of God's holiness in terms of his absolute righteousness, his perfect love, and his complete knowledge. But let's think for a moment about these three terms. If I were to ask you to give me a good definition for each of them, you could probably do so. But what is a definition? Merely a series of words that equals another word.

It is personal experience, not words, that lead us to truly comprehend what a term means. For instance, where in your experience—outside of God himself—do you find anything you can compare with his righteousness, his perfect love, or his absolute knowledge? No such thing exists. Therefore, terms and their definitions will never be sufficient.

Perhaps the best description of holiness is that it is *a concentration of love so intense that it becomes like a consuming*

fire. In a world that is unholy by nature—resolutely incon-
sistent, unrighteous, unjust, and unloving—this is one of
the most difficult concepts for us to grasp. To help us
understand, God gave us "pictures" of holiness that we
could see and touch. Consider, for example, the picture of
the burning bush.

Moses was in the hill country caring for his sheep, just
minding his own business. Then out of the corner of his eye
he caught sight of a remarkable thing—a bush was engulfed
in flames. Now, a bush burning in the desert wasn't all that
amazing a sight. The really astonishing thing was that the
bush burned and burned, yet it was not consumed. When
Moses went over to get a closer look, God called down to
him, "Take off your sandals, Moses, for you are standing on
holy ground."

Holy ground? It was just a piece of desert sand surround-
ing a scraggly bush. Ah, but that's the point. The ground
was *made* holy by the divine presence of God. It was consecrated to his service, separated from the commonplace.
Because God was using it, it was holy ground.

There were many other pictures given in Old Testament
times, too: the setting apart of the nation of Israel as a holy
people, the tabernacle with its Holy of Holies set aside as
God's abode, the establishment of a holy priesthood, the
wondrous temple in Jerusalem—all these were pictures that
paved the way for us finally to see Holiness personified in
the person of Jesus Christ. He was the living Tabernacle,
the Son of God, the High Priest for all humankind, and the
perfect sacrifice.

Without the pictures, we could never begin to comprehend holiness. And without comprehension, we can never find the openness which will allow God the Father to reveal himself to us so that we may know him and his great glory.

Grace

Grace is another word we need to see to believe. It has been defined as the "unmerited favor of God toward people, necessary for their salvation." Grace is not a two-way word. It comes uniquely *from* God and goes *to* man. In Ephesians 2:8-9 we read: "For it is by grace you have been saved, through faith—and this not from yourselves, it is the gift of God—not by works, so that no one can boast."

Sounds simple, doesn't it? Well, yes and no. The language barrier tends to cause us to think that grace either means we have the license to do anything we want to do, or that the grace is conditional (a real contradiction in terms!). In *The Cost of Discipleship*, Dietrich Bonhoeffer describes cheap grace as "grace without discipleship, grace without the Cross, grace without Jesus Christ, living and incarnate."[2] This kind of grace plays at life. Nothing is taken very seriously; nothing has any real value.

Jerry was a proponent of easy grace. He had carefully fashioned his life through a series of choices designed to take care of "number one"—himself.

Even after Jerry married and became a father, the rules that governed his life did not change. He did what he wanted when he wanted to do it, and he made decisions with little concern or regard for his family or anyone else. When he cashed in his retirement benefits and bought himself an expensive new sports car, he simply grinned, shrugged his shoulders, and told his furious wife, "Guess it's a good thing I'm covered by God's grace!"

Cheap grace would have us believe that nothing really matters. It says that people and things are to be used for our own personal pleasure, and that the cost of that use is unimportant. Cheap grace knows nothing about truth, honor, responsibility, and integrity. It preaches forgiveness that comes with an easy, "I'm sorry," but that never really touches the heart and causes repentance. Cheap grace frowns on discipline or punishment, and does not take seriously the meaning and cost of discipleship.

Cheap grace means limited grace. Even though our experience tries to tell us otherwise, there is no such thing. True grace is always unmerited, always undeserved, always unwarranted. And outside personal experience with God, it is always unknown. Sure, we can strive toward grace in our relationships with other people, but if we are realistic and honest, we will have to admit that true grace is something we are never really able to achieve.

Yet our experience of receiving grace from God is the doorway that opens us up to all he has for us. It is the foundation of our faith. It is what gives us our sense of security in the midst of our struggles, our fears, and our failures.

Justification

To understand justification, imagine this picture: God has requested you to appear before him. Perfectly aware of the desperation of your situation, the thought of meeting the Holy God face to face terrifies you. You are overwhelmed by the flood of guilt from your sin. You are paralyzed with fear because of your shame and condemnation.

As you stand trembling, a gentle voice calls out, "Come to me." The invitation penetrates into the very depths of your being, and you hesitantly stumble your way to the foot of the cross. Yet the unbearable burden of your sin and shame prevents you from looking upward into the voice that beckoned you.

Just when you feel the most helpless, Jesus' hands cup your chin and lift up your head. You look into his eyes; they are filled with such compassion. The amazing thing is that even though he can see right into the center of your being, even though the awful blackness and ugliness of your sin is right there before him, his look of love is unfaltering.

In an instant the sin and blackness, shame and despair, disappear from your soul. Jesus has taken them upon himself. In their place he gives you love and hope and light. Your sin-filled heart is spotlessly clean. Now you can stand before God, consecrated, holy, and blameless. And why? For one reason alone—you said yes to God's invitation to come to him.

But the picture doesn't end there. A robe of purple and gold is placed upon you. Clothed in his righteousness, you are now a full-fledged member of his own royal family. Then Jesus Christ beckons you to follow, and he leads you into the presence of the King of the Universe.

"Father," he says as he introduces you, "here is your long-awaited child!"

Wow! What a picture!

Guess what? This is a picture of reality; it is the actual portrait of justification. Accepting God's gift of salvation, provided through the death of his Son Jesus Christ, makes it more than "just as if I had never sinned." Justification means that Christ's very righteousness has been credited to me by the Holy God.

 More than anything else, justification will lead us to a sense of being pleasing to God. Was it not the Father who declared of Christ and his righteousness, "This is my beloved Son in whom I am well pleased"? It is not our *behavior* but our *person* that pleases God. The more we experience being pleasing to our Heavenly Father, the more our behavior will reflect who he made us to be.

One of my great joys as a father is seeing my children enjoying me as their daddy. How it would hurt me to know they were unhappy about being my children. If this is true of earthly fathers, how much more it must grieve our Heavenly Father to see his children missing out on experiencing his love and his pleasure in them.

Sin

"Sure, I supplied my home office with pens and paper clips and other office materials from work," Dana admitted. "Maybe it wasn't the best thing to do, even though everyone else takes stuff home, too. But since I'm a Christian, I guess it was a mistake."

"The reason I got involved with the woman at work was that I was under a great deal of pressure and my wife wasn't there for me," Carl explained. "It was an error in judgment on my part."

A mistake? An error in judgment? That's not what God calls the transgression of his laws. He calls it sin.

I don't think there is any word that has taken more of a beating in our culture than sin. Movies enact situations that would have been unthinkable just a few years ago. Television talk shows parade depravity as simple "lifestyle variations." Infidelity, divorce, domestic violence, substance abuse—these are a part of everyday life in our society. It is to our great detriment that we now consider sin to be a relative term. *If enough people do it,* we reason, *then it must not really be sin at all. It's just a reflection of the progressive nature of man.*

Even in the lives of God's children, we see evidence of evil embraced with absolute fatalism. The person who harbors intense hatred and anger, the one who tolerates prejudice and racism, the individual who spreads rumors and conflict, the one who disdains a brother who has fallen and is struggling to make it to his feet—we in the Christian community are much more ready to reject the *people* than to reject the *evil* they represent.

Even more subtle is our readiness to cast sin as merely the breaking of a rule. Our lives are full of rules. Some of them are for our own good, others are for the benefit of others. Either way, human rules seem important only if we suffer consequences for breaking them. If there is no immediate consequence for being late to work, for instance, we come in late more and more often, and don't really worry about it (at least until we are passed over for a promotion due to our tardiness!). Soon we begin to see God's rules as no different from all the other rules in our lives. We do not see the reality of sin until we begin to suffer its consequences.

The apostle Paul teaches that sin is a ruling principle of

human life; it is part of our nature. In Romans 3:23 we read, "For all have sinned and fall short of the glory of God." And that's not all. In Romans 6:23 we are warned, "For the wages of sin is death, but the gift of God is eternal life in Christ Jesus our Lord."

Sin is the acting out of evil. I know, I know. We have reserved the term "evil" for only the most horrendous of crimes. But the truth is that all sin is evil, because it carves a destructive path through our lives. Our numbness to this destruction makes it no less devastating. It is precisely because of the ravages of evil that we are instructed to "work out our salvation with fear and trembling." The Holy Spirit has come into our lives to warn us of the impending destruction before we suffer sin's full impact.

To have a heart knowledge of what sin really means, you must allow the Holy Spirit to show you its destructive ways in your life.

Forgiveness

Pretty sorry picture of us humans, isn't it? We fail. We hurt people. We offend others. We let them down. And because other people are human beings, they fail us, too. That's why forgiveness is such an important concept to us. To be forgiven means that the failure has been erased. It's as though it never occurred. We can go back to where we were before we failed and start over again.

To a degree, people do forgive one another. But human forgiveness is a pale shadow of the true forgiveness God offers us. True forgiveness is linked directly with Christ and rooted in the graciousness of God. It rests in the atoning work of Jesus. Matthew 26:28 tells us that Christ's blood was shed "for many for the forgiveness of sins." Yet God's forgiveness is personal for each one of us. Ephesians 4:32 instructs us to forgive each other, "just as in Christ God forgave you."

We glibly tell each other, "Yes, I forgive you," often adding under our breath, "although I'm not about to forget what you did!" Even while we're insisting that we are forgiving, we are busy "getting even." Because that has always been our human experience, deep in our hearts we believe that part of God's forgiveness is that he will get even with us. We say we know his forgiveness, yet we look at the troubles in our lives and suspect that God is actually meting out his vengeance on us.

Even when we truly want to "forgive and forget," we are incapable of doing it. Not so with God. When he forgives, he literally wipes the past from our lives. He removes our sins from us for all eternity. The psalmist tells us, "As far as the east is from the west, so far has he removed our transgressions from us" (Psalm 103:12).

When Jesus says, "Friend, your sins are forgiven," we are free indeed. Where in our human experience can we find such forgiveness? Nowhere but in God.

Obedience

Out of our relationships we have defined what obedience means: someone has power over us, and we do what they tell us to because we are afraid of their authority. That's exactly how most Christians see God. He has the power, and he sets the rules. They may be capricious rules, they may be designed to benefit him instead of us, but we have to go along with them, because if we step out of line, we get zapped.

At best, this view of obedience leads us to a sense of resentment for everything we are missing out on. At the worst, it leads to total rebellion against God.

This isn't the picture Scripture gives us of obedience. In Romans 8:1 we read, "Therefore, there is now no condemnation to those who are in Christ Jesus." Look at it this way: Imagine yourself in a burning building. Desperately you grope your way along the wall, searching for a way out, but the smoke is so thick you can see nothing. Just when everything looks hopeless, a fireman grabs your hand and cries, "Follow me!" What are you going to do? Obey and follow? Or resist and die?

That's how it is with God. His rules and his leading have one purpose—to bring us into life. Unfortunately, because of our misunderstanding of obedience, we don't "get it."

Regeneration

The word *regeneration* means to be reborn, actually to reemerge as a new person. When we are regenerated, we gain a new bloodline, a whole new family. We literally become children of God.

No change we know compares to our regeneration. A butterfly may look totally different from the caterpillar it once was, but it's really just the same thing in a changed form. A frog is really just a tadpole in a different body. Everything we know that appears to be radically changed, is really just the same old thing in a different form. But when

God changes us, we are *really changed*. He reaches deep down inside of us to the very essence of our beings and makes of us an entirely new creation.

Unlike the butterfly or the frog, your regenerated self looks no different on the outside, but your spirit *is* new. That old spirit you were born with, the one which had no hope of ever communing with God, has been done away with and a new spirit has been put in its place. The Holy Spirit himself has taken up residence inside you. With his leading and power, even the strongest evil forces in creation cannot overcome you. One moment you were a servant of sin, the next you have ultimate victory over all evil.

The only way regeneration can ever become more than just a word defined by more words is for you to experience it for yourself.

Peace

What is peace? Most people describe it by stating what it is not: peace is the absence of war, of conflict, of anxiety, of chaos. But to the Christian, peace takes on a whole new and challenging meaning. For us, peace exists in the very midst of war and conflict and anxiety and chaos.

God's peace surpasses the limitation of language. We have all experienced the relief of having a difficult situation work out. We know what it is to be worried about a child who is in rebellion, then to suddenly see that child's life turn around. We understand what it is to have an illness, and then to get well. But peace is much more than just relief. It doesn't occur in the midst of our struggles simply-because we discover a solution to our problem. It occurs because we *re*discover a sweetness in our relationship with God. The peace God gives will always be a part of our relationship, and only secondarily because we are relieved about a specific situation.

In Israel, Jews greet one another with shouts of "Shalom!" We translate this wonderful word as "peace," but it is peace at its absolute fullest. Shalom means wholeness and salvation. It means being truly one with yourself, with your neighbor, and with God. Not only is it an expression of well being for the individual, it embraces the whole community right in the midst of its busy life.

For us as Christians, peace encompasses all the meaning of "shalom," but it includes an even richer spiritual dimension. For us it encompasses the grace and righteousness of God that can only be obtained through Jesus Christ. It is the assurance of a "hope and a future" that reaches beyond this world and throughout eternity. With this eternal perspective, we can view the turmoil and crises of life in a whole new way.

The greatest obstacle to our experiencing peace is our willingness to accept something far less than what our Father wants for us. We live in Colorado where the winds can rip through the mountains at more than seventy miles per hour, churning up the mountain lakes in their wake. Then without warning, the winds suddenly stop. Without even the slightest breeze to disturb it, the water becomes like a mirror reflecting the grand mountains on every side.

When we find peace, we will move from the roaring billows of life to dwell beside the still waters in which his majesty is reflected.

All other barriers between our heads and our hearts are

constructed on the foundation of the language barrier. No wonder it is the hardest of all for us to overcome. Only when we have a more precise picture of what we mean by a specific word are we ready to confront the next biggest barrier—our past experiences.

know who you are in God

Questions for Reflection and Discussion

1. How can our frame of reference or the use of comparison help to distort Christian words and concepts?

2. Little Amanda's parents had a formula for life: if they did everything right, all would be well. They had indeed done everything "right," but their precious little daughter had died tragically. We told you that their "why" question lured them into a trap of trying to understand God versus trying to know him. What is the difference between the two? Why is trying to understand God such a deadly trap?

3. Have you ever had to face such a tragic situation? How did you handle it? What barriers did you encounter along the way?

4. When we try to describe God's attributes, we immediately face a dilemma. Even if we can describe one attribute, we suddenly realize that we must somehow hold several together at one time—attributes such as omnipotence and omniscience, holiness and love. These words

almost seem to contradict one another, and the dilemma is created! How could we use language to help us create comfortable boxes for these difficult concepts and avoid the dilemma?

5. Jerry was invested in taking care of himself. Even his spiritual language helped to give him the excuses he needed. How does his use of the word "grace" create a barrier between himself and God?

6. Ask several people to define the word sin. If you have children, ask them. What is your definition? What do you notice about your variety of definitions? How do these definitions differ from scriptural definitions? What does this tell you about the way we use language as a barrier?

1. Davis, Ronald D. *The Gift of Dyslexia* (Ability Workshop Press, 1994).
2. Bonhoeffer, Dietrich. *The Cost of Discipleship* (New York: MacMillian Publishing, 1995).

THREE

BARRIER #2: EXPERIENCE

"**I** don't know how I feel about God!" a young woman named Charlotte exclaimed to me. Talented, attractive, and successful in her career, she was really struggling with Philippians 2:10, which states: "At the name of Jesus, every knee shall bow, in heaven and on earth and under the earth."

"What gives God the right to demand that I bow down to him?" she exclaimed. "It's like he has this huge ego, and he just has to see us do tricks like a bunch of trained seals. I won't serve a God who makes people bow down to him!"

Charlotte's objection seemed awfully odd to me. What was her problem, anyway? How could she talk about the God of the universe so disrespectfully?

As I talked to Charlotte, I began to understand where the problem lay. She had no grasp of the authority of God. Unfortunately, Charlotte is not alone. The world is full of people who reject God's authority in their lives.

Charlotte had been raised by an overbearing father who always had to have the last word about everything. No one could tell him anything, and he would not allow any argument. "He was always ordering us kids around," Charlotte told me. "I couldn't wait to get away from the house and out from under his domineering thumb!"

Charlotte's experience told her that if she allowed someone to be in authority over her, that person would take advantage of the position. That's how it had been with her father, and that's how it must surely be with God. Her experience created an impenetrable barrier that kept God away from his rightful place in her life. It was a vicious circle. Without God in the place of authority, Charlotte was left to manage life on her own. When things happened that she couldn't understand, all she could do was turn back to God and defiantly announce, "See? I knew he couldn't be counted on!"

Tim had another reason for challenging God's authority: he didn't like God's rules.

It had all started innocently enough. Tim simply enjoyed the company of Candace, a co-worker. They had a good working relationship. Nothing wrong with that. As their friendship grew, they began to confide in one another. Actually, they had a great deal in common, including their frustration that their spouses didn't understand them. Somehow their friendship moved to what Tim was convinced was true love. He never referred to his relationship with Candace as an "affair." That had too sordid a sound for the "love" they shared.

"God understands my situation," Tim insisted to me. "He sent Candace and me to each other at just the right time."

Tim was totally blind to God's instructions forbidding

adultery. He knew the facts, but those facts didn't balance with his experience. In the end, he allowed experience to win out.

THE PAST COMES BACK

Our experience barriers arise from painful or powerful experiences in our past that live on, negatively affecting our view of the present. The experience may have been a single event, or it may have been a series of events. Either way, along with the experience comes a message that generally either contradicts God's Word or what we know of his character. Oftentimes we find that our understanding of "truth," or our most deeply held beliefs, are defined by the experiences we have had.

"But good or bad, my experiences are my experiences," you may be saying. "If they create a barrier to my view of reality, what can I do about it? I mean, I can't even see a barrier there, much less work at removing it!"

Don't be so sure. God knows all about our barriers, and it is his desire to reveal them to us and enable us to bring them down. When I (Rujon) invited God into my sleepless night, he brought my unresolved feeling of abandonment to my mind. I had buried that unhappy event so deeply that I didn't even know it existed, but he dug it up and laid bare my distrust and disbelief. He exposed that "heart message" for what it was: an experience barrier that had been quietly but relentlessly challenging the character of God and the power of his Word.

HOW DO THESE BARRIERS WORK?

Let's look at our eight words and see some of the ways experience barriers can grow up and block the way between our heads and our hearts.

Holy

Corrine was raised in a church that stressed praising God out loud. Their music consisted of catchy tunes that spoke of God in lighthearted ditties, and easy platitudes flowed freely, both from the pulpit and between the worshippers.

"Prayer and praise are just a natural part of my everyday life," Corrine told me blithely. I could see what she meant. A real estate salesperson, she told me about how she handled her transactions: "If a client seems at all interested in a property, I take his or her hand, close my eyes and pray out loud, 'God, make this sale happen if it's your will!' Then I exclaim, 'Praise the Lord!' Some clients don't like it, but that's their problem. I have to praise God in *all* things!"

Praise is good, and it is right. But it is also possible for a specific manner of praise to create an experience barrier. In Corrine's church, the word "holy" loses a great deal of its power by being trivialized. In our effort to make God an approachable buddy, we can end up robbing him of his awesome holiness.

Other churches fall into the trap of allowing objects to become the *focus* of holiness rather than a way of leading us to an understanding of Christ. Church altars, celebration of the sacraments, the music, public prayers, the cross displayed, the stained glass windows—we must never allow any of these to become our focus instead of God's holiness.

One final warning: Because we want what we want, we define God's holiness down to where it will accept our behavior. As Tim did, we convince ourselves that since nothing catastrophic has happened to us, God's holiness is willing to tolerate whatever we are doing. This is a dangerous deception.

Grace

From the time she was tiny, whenever Lauren would misbehave, her mother would scold, "You are a bad girl! You are a bad, bad girl!" With that pronouncement, little Lauren would be banished to her room to think about how terrible she was. "And you can stay there," her mother would order, "until you say you're sorry!"

Now, Lauren was a smart child. It didn't take her long to learn to say the right words. As soon as she "confessed" she would be released from her room with a stern warning not to be bad again. That's all—no hugs, no reassurance, no expressions of love or acceptance, just a stern warning.

Lauren learned the lesson well: people who made mistakes were bad, unlovable, and they deserved to be punished. Love had to be earned by being good. Trouble was, she never managed to be good enough. She tried and tried, but she always ended up doing something wrong and ruining everything.

Now thirty-two years old, Lauren cannot understand why she can't have a meaningful relationship with anyone—not even a close friendship. Why can't she find someone who measures up to her expectations? Surely there is *someone* else who truly wants to be good.

Lauren can quote the theological definition of grace: "It means unmerited favor," she told me. Yet she is completely unable to apply the principle of grace to her own life. Because of her childhood experiences, Lauren has no frame of reference for unconditional love.

Justification

Stan is a new believer. He is so excited about the Lord that he cannot contain himself. "I'm an entirely new person!" he exclaims to everyone he meets. "I now know God on a personal level. In his eyes, I am perfect. My sins have been removed!"

The reactions to Stan's excitement are varied. Seasoned Christians tend to smile and shake their heads indulgently. "It will wear off," they murmur. "Give him time. He'll get his feet back on the ground." Some people simply stare at him with a blank expression. Some argue with him. Now and then, someone will laugh in his face. But there are those few who catch his enthusiasm and say, "You've really got something, Stan. I want to know more about it."

All these people are hearing the same story from the same new believer. So what accounts for the different reactions? To a large degree, it is based on a person's past experience. Christians who have lost touch with where they came from forget how truly wondrous it is to be justified. Those who don't accept their sinful condition and their need for a Savior have no frame of reference. They can't understand. But those whose hearts have been made tender by the Holy Spirit are open to experiencing justification first hand.

It is up to us as Christians to be living models of the power of justification. What a rewarding challenge!

Sin

Pastor Sam Reeves had been at the church for two years, and the congregation had nothing but praise for him. The church had almost doubled in size since he came. His teaching was exceptional and his knowledge of the Scriptures was incredible. He had even started a counseling center—something the congregation had long anticipated. In fact, many would have pointed to his counseling skills as the most vital part of his ministry.

It just so happened that Pastor Reeves' counseling clients were mostly women. What no one knew was that he had become sexually involved with several of them. The situation came to light when one of the women confided to a friend about her "special relationship" with the pastor. It just so happened that her friend also had a "special relationship."

Rather than asking Pastor Reeves to leave the church, the elders suggested he take a leave of absence and go through therapy with a trained Christian counselor. To their surprise, he refused.

"Why do you have to make such a big deal out of this?" he insisted.

The church had no choice but to let Pastor Reeves go. He responded by starting another church nearby. To this day, Sam Reeves will not admit that what he did was sin.

When our sin is not immediately punished, experience teaches us that God is indifferent to our actions. We come to believe he doesn't really care what we do. That's why it is so important that we heed the Holy Spirit's warnings. If we turn our backs and defiantly follow our own way, our hearts can become so hardened that we no longer recognize our sin.

Forgiveness

Because complete forgiveness is impossible for humans to achieve, most of us harbor some forgiveness barriers from our pasts. Here is how they show themselves in the lives of Cheryl and Ron:

If you have a job to do, Cheryl is the person you want working beside you. She is thorough, dependable, and never seems to run out of energy. Your biggest problem will likely be guilt—you just won't be able to keep up with her! Sounds great, doesn't she? Actually, what you are seeing is an experience barrier in action. For Cheryl, *doing* outweighs *being*. She is forever striving to be "good enough" to earn God's forgiveness.

Ron's relationship with God could best be described as one of frustration. "My whole life, I've tried so hard to be worthy of God's forgiveness," he says with a sigh. "I honestly think I have done all the right things, but I still feel empty inside. Where is all that joy I'm supposed to have?"

If we feel we need to earn our own forgiveness, we cannot accept it freely. We cannot forgive others. If we cannot forgive others, we live a life of torment and anger. Alienated and alone, we will look at whatever happens to us and interpret it as further proof that we are unworthy and that God is just getting back at us.

Obedience

I (Rujon) was driving down the interstate the other day and noticed that the cars were all moving along together, not a single one going faster than the posted speed limit. Now, that's a rare sight! I soon saw the reason for the mass obedience. There was a marked police car up ahead going the speed limit, and no one dared pass him. A few miles further on, the police car exited and everyone immediately picked up speed. But a few miles further, there was another police car. You guessed it. Brake lights came on all around me and I was again surrounded by law-abiding citizens.

Many of us learned our approach to obedience as young children. Mommy said, "Don't touch that!" and we didn't—until Mommy was out of sight, that is. Teacher said, "Don't talk in class," and we didn't—until her back was turned. Often, our approach worked. We learned that authority has a limited vision.

Now we tend to relate to God just as we related to those other authority figures—we obey him as long we think he can see what we are doing. Our obedience is limited by what we think we can get away with.

Regeneration

Charlie could not believe where he was. He remembered going out for a few drinks with some guys from work—just to be sociable and relax. He hadn't intended to drink so much. Actually, alcohol had been a problem for him for a long time, but recently he had gotten it under control. But now here he was, in a hotel room with some strange woman, and he had no idea how he had gotten here. How could this have happened?

Only a few weeks earlier, Charlie was in a totally different place and situation. Some friends had taken him to breakfast, and they had all spent hours talking about what really mattered in life. At the end of their time together, Charlie had prayed, asking Christ into his life. He enjoyed attending church with his friends, and he seemed to be growing in the Lord. Charlie truly felt like the "new creation" his friends told him he was.

And now here he was. "Maybe the old things haven't changed after all," he lamented to himself. "Maybe even God can't make a new creature out of the likes of me."

Part of the experience barrier that bars us from understanding regeneration can be laid at the feet of well-meaning members of the Christian community. We lead each other to believe that since our spirits are new, our bodies and characters and habits and personalities should also be immediately renewed. We think every problem should be solved overnight. When it doesn't happen that way, we question the validity of God's work in our lives—or in the lives of those around us.

Peace

"Sometimes a thunderbolt, as men call it, will shoot from a clear sky; and sometimes, into the midst of a peaceful family, or yet a quieter individuality, without warning of gathered storm above or slightest tremble of earthquake beneath, will fall a terrible fact, and from that moment everything has changed. That family or life is no more what it was—probably never more can be what it was. Better it ought to be, worse it may be—which depends upon itself. But its spiritual weather is altered. The air is thick with cloud, and cannot weep itself clear. There may come a gorgeous sunset, though."[1]

I (Rujon) had only just read this quote from George MacDonald when the telephone call came. My forty-one-year-old brother, Trent, had asked a doctor to check out a cough that wouldn't go away. The x-ray results were startling; there was a tumor the size of a walnut in his left lung. Trent's response to the doctor was, "OK then, Doctor, we'll just take that lung out. I'm healthy. I can get along fine with one lung!" The doctor wasn't so sure. He ordered more tests.

Several days later our family's own earthquake came. Trent was diagnosed with a rare form of cancer, and it had progressed from his left lung into a lymph node. That wasn't all; the tumor sat right against the pulmonary artery, and unless it could be shrunk there wasn't even hope for an operation. We were absolutely devastated. The ground dropped out from under us.

How can we possibly experience peace in the midst of personal catastrophe? When we are threatened with financial ruin? When we are enduring illness and suffering, even death? How can we experience peace when we are too numb from agonizing pain to even think rationally? Our experiences bar us from considering the possibility of a "peace that passes understanding." Our experience insists:

- "God's vision is limited."

- "God should have done a better job when he created me."

- "I am not lovable."

- "My problems are too great for God to handle."

- "I can't shake my bad habits."

- "God can't be counted on."

We cannot depend upon our experience for accurate guidance. Only faith can prevent us from stumbling on this barrier. And that faith must be founded upon fact and truth. Otherwise we will be tripped up by barrier #3: our distorted beliefs.

Questions for Reflection and Discussion

1. Tim's experience with Candace left him sure that they shared true love. How did Tim's "experience" create a heart barrier which kept him from receiving God's word?

2. Corrine's experience in the church taught her that God would hear her and answer her prayers if she praised him out loud. Her training left her with a spiritual rule to live by, one that actually trivialized God. Can you think of personal experiences where you learned lessons about God's character or how you are supposed to live the Christian life? What kinds of barriers do these "rules" create between you and God's truth?

3. Hebrews 3:8 says, "Do not harden your hearts as you did in the rebellion...." How does this Scripture fit with Pastor Sam Reeves and the experiences he found himself in with the women he counseled and the elders who warned him of his sin? How does rebellion strengthen and solidify a barrier of experience?

4. Experiencing unconditional love and being able to receive this gift is a prerequisite to having the ability to forgive others (read the parable of the unmerciful servant in Matthew 18: 21-35).

   Think about Cheryl's situation: she is forever striving to be "good enough" to deserve God's love and forgiveness. How has her experience of conditional love created a barrier to receive a heart encounter with God's love?

5. Storms and earthquakes strike when we least expect them. Trent's diagnosis of cancer came with a force that knocked the ground out from under Rujon's family. Trent was only forty-one. They had lost their forty-seven-year-old father when they were just teenagers. The family seemed to be reliving a nightmare. Over the next few months there were many times when God seemed so distant and the only message Rujon could hear was that of the barriers. Their powerful messages constantly tested her faith in God.

   What barriers have been created in your life from "storms" and "earthquakes" that have hit unawares? What do their messages say about God and his character? How do these messages rob you of the peace God has for you?

6. What key Scriptures have sustained you during times of turmoil? How have they come against the barriers? Spend some time reflecting on these.

---

1. Neuhouser, David L., comp. *George MacDonald: Selections from His Greatest Works 1824-1905* (Wheaton, IL: Scripture Press, 1990), 25.

FOUR

BARRIER #3:
DISTORTED BELIEFS

It has been said that God gave us rules to live by, and that people have been adding to the list ever since. There is a lot of truth in this.

Eileen knows all about that inflated list. Her childhood was consumed with attempts to keep up with rules. She wasn't allowed to celebrate any holidays (they weren't Christ-centered). She couldn't have her hair cut (an Old Testament prohibition). She could only wear dresses (something about not compromising her womanhood). She could not watch television or go to movies (sinful worldly influences). She would never even dare utter such carnal words as "wine" and "dance." The list of rules went on and on. Although Eileen long ago turned her back on the legalism of her childhood, she cannot seem to shake the need to adhere to lists of rules.

Andy's take on rules is different. He was taught that God was a being so supreme that he could never be bothered with the trivial concerns of everyday folks; God has no interest in the personal details of people's lives. Because this is what Andy's heart believes, he never takes his concerns to

God. He never gives God a chance to prove his personal concern.

Tell Eileen and Andy all you want about the truth of God's love. The information can't reach their hearts because of the strong barrier of their distorted belief.

IT REALLY DOES MATTER WHAT YOU BELIEVE

Even though our brains know that the distorted beliefs are erroneous, our hearts insist on accepting them as truth. Let's look at our eight words and see how this barrier can block both our desire and our ability to know God.

Holy

Nathan worked hard at being the kind of Christian he thought he should be. He had grown up attending Sunday School and church, and had a degree from a well-known Bible college. Nathan had an answer for everything, and his answers were accompanied by a list of rules on how to live a godly life.

"When I was a child, the movie theater was my greatest temptation," Nathan recalls. "More than once, I sneaked away from home and into a theater to watch a movie. That was considered extremely sinful in our religious circle. I remember sitting there terrified that Jesus would come back and find me, and then that he would bar me from heaven forever. But I loved the movies so much that I'd swallow my fear and go anyway."

Nathan insisted that he had a good grasp on the holiness

of God. He saw God as a strict teacher with a grade book in one hand and a ruler in the other, just waiting to catch his students' mistakes so he could put checks by their names and give them a punishing whack. Not surprisingly, Nathan worried constantly about accumulating too many "checks." What would happen then? Why, God might actually erase his name from the Book of Life!

Nathan had grown up questioning whether or not God really wanted him to make it into heaven. He had lived in constant fear that he would not be good enough to be acceptable. And now, so many years later, he was still shouldering the responsibility of making sure he would deserve an eternity in heaven.

In our attempt to become a holy people, we too often fall into the distorted belief that keeping lists of do's and don'ts will prove us righteous. This trap binds us into a system of "doing" that strives to overrule what Christ has already done for us. As we live out this distorted belief, we cannot help but become rigid, critical, and judgmental of ourselves and others. In the process, we totally miss God's gift of unconditional love and acceptance.

Dave also believes God's holiness is wrapped up in his own works, but unlike Nathan, he is not afraid. In fact, Dave is totally confident. Like a surprising—and growing—number of Christians today, he firmly believes that if he prays hard enough, and if he does enough good things, God is obligated to give him whatever his heart desires. It's almost a God-is-my-puppet theology, and its popularity is growing. Right now Dave is praying for a new top-of-the-line Mercedes-Benz with all the extras.

"I'm proving my faith by building a special garage for my new car," Dave says confidently. "God will grant me my desire. He has to!"

Bernie's view of God's holiness is just the opposite. "God's power?" he asks sarcastically. "What's that? Listen, I've been around long enough to know that if anyone is going to watch out for me, it's me myself. I work hard to pay my own way and take care of my family. When I need something, either I get it for myself or I do without it. When I'm sick, I take myself to the doctor—and I pay the bills. When problems arise, I handle them. That's the bottom line fact of the matter."

What about the miracles so many of us have experienced? "Miracles?" Bernie snorts. "You show me a miracle, and I'll show you an event that has a logical explanation. The only miracles in my life are the ones I make happen."

Nathan, Dave, and Bernie all have strong views about the holiness of God. Unfortunately, their beliefs are tragically distorted.

Grace

"God is gracious," Dave says confidently. "He is *so* gracious that he wants us to be happy."

Really? Is our happiness the measure of God's grace? Listen to this tale of two families:

The Kincaids and the Lambertis had been friends for years. They lived in the same neighborhood, were active in the same church, and their children were the same ages. One Labor Day, the two families were celebrating the last holiday of summer together at the Lambertis' house. As the

four adults busied themselves getting the hamburgers bar-
becued and corn on the cob and potato salad on the table,
the six children splashed around in the pool. At least, the
parents *thought* all the kids were in the pool. Actually the
older ones had gone out front to play football, leaving the
two little ones alone.

No one is quite sure what happened. Evidently three-
year-old Alex Lamberti and two-year-old Emily Kincaid
decided to climb aboard a plastic floating raft, but it tipped
over and dumped them into the pool. What they do know
is that Joyce Kincaid came out to call the children to dinner
and found the two little ones lying on the bottom of the
pool. Two frantic hours later, the families sat together in the
hospital waiting room and listened in shocked horror as the
doctor gave them the news: Emily would recover, but Alex
had died.

Had the Kincaids experienced more of God's grace than
the Lambertis? Was their faith stronger? Had they prayed
harder? Some would say so. But such distorted beliefs about
the nature of God's grace removes his sovereignty from the
situation. It assumes that we, mere human beings, are able
to know the mind of God and to understand his will.

Justification

Glen had a passion for people who had not heard the
good news of the gospel. He started a downtown mission
organization where he preached justification by faith in
Jesus Christ. The ministry grew quickly. Before long Glen
became known for his dedication to the down-and-out pop-
ulation, and for his determination to make a real difference

in their lives. With more and more responsibility turned over to him, Glen quickly advanced to a prominent position in the city.

Year after year, Glen's achievements grew. Whenever there was a challenge, he would meet it. Whenever there was a problem, he would solve it. Whenever there was a question, he was the one with the answer. In time, everyone began to expect Glen to take care of everything. Without realizing it, he was teaching his team to put their trust in him.

As time went on, Glen began to feel increasingly empty inside. The responsibilities overwhelmed him. "Everyone uses me," he complained to his wife. "Everything falls onto my shoulders. Everything is my responsibility. I have to do it all."

But Glen's real despair was the crushing feeling that he was letting God down. "I feel like I'm on a spiritual treadmill, and I just don't know what to do about it," he said in despair. "I'm torn between jumping off and giving it all up, and hanging on and sinking to sure destruction. Either way, I lose."

Although Glen preached justification by faith, his own life proved he was clinging to the distorted belief that *he* was the one who had to do the saving. The salvation of the city, and his own justification, was his responsibility. He was the savior.

Distorted belief tells us it is up to us to do the saving.

Sin

Nothing had gone right for Yvonne that morning. It was always hard to get her five children dressed, fed, and out of the house on time, but with an important 8:00 A.M. appointment of her own, this day was a special challenge. Yvonne had just dropped off her two youngest kids at school when she noticed a police car following her, its lights flashing.

When Yvonne pulled over, the officer approached her and pointed to the stop sign she had just driven through.

"I'm really sorry," Yvonne said. Then she hastened to explain, "It's been one of those mornings, Officer, and I just didn't see the sign." She flashed her most engaging smile and added, "I'm really a very good driver. I've never even had a ticket. Wouldn't you let it go this one time?"

He would not.

"Lady, whether you saw it or not, the stop sign is right there," the officer said. "You didn't stop, you broke the law. Here's your ticket."

No excuses, no explanations, no apologies.

Distorted belief tells us that if we don't recognize an action as sin, if we do something without thinking or without malice, if our intentions are good, if there are extenuating circumstances, then it doesn't count as sin. Distorted belief tells us we can fool God.

Forgiveness

It had been almost a year since Suzanne had had her abortion. She had met regularly with a counselor, and together they had dealt with all sorts of things. Still, Suzanne just couldn't get over the horrible feelings inside her. She visited her pastor numerous times, and they prayed together. Months ago he had led her in a prayer of repentance and confession.

"But how can I really *know* I'm forgiven?" she puzzled. "I don't *feel* forgiven."

When her church started operating a hot line for women considering abortion, Suzanne thought she had found her answer. She would volunteer to help work the telephone. Surely then she would be forgiven.

After Suzanne volunteered for the sixth night straight, the supervising counselor took her aside. "Why are you doing this, Suzanne?" she asked.

"Because I want to help," Suzanne told her. "I know how it feels to be on the other side of that phone line, and I want to be there for women who need me."

But the counselor persisted: "Are you sure that's all there is to it?" Then she quickly added, "We appreciate your help, Suzanne, but I can't help but feel there is something more to it."

There was. Suzanne was deluded by the distorted belief that reality is based on feelings. If she didn't feel forgiven, then surely she couldn't be. She was trying to work her way through to the feeling.

Confusing *the fact of forgiveness* with *feeling forgiven* is a common barrier. Consider Jay and Brian. When Jay disagreed with the position Brian took on a minor church issue, he lost no time in letting Brian know how he felt. *Stupid*, *fool*, and *asinine* are just a few of the words Jay chose to throw at his friend and Christian brother. After he cooled down, he apologized and asked Brian to forgive him. Brian said he would, and they shook hands.

"Well, I'm glad that's over," Jay said.

Both Brian and Jay wanted things to be back the way

they were. But they weren't. Every time Brian saw his former close friend, the words *stupid* and *fool* and *asinine* rang in his ears.

Like Brian and Jay, many Christians have been taught that when we forgive one another we should immediately be in a right relationship with that other person. If we are not reconciled, then the forgiveness couldn't have been real.

Believing that forgiveness always means reconciliation is another distorted belief that often gets in the way of forgiveness.

Obedience

The hardest day in Rosemary and Louis' life had to be the day the doctor told them something was terribly wrong with their unborn baby. "I strongly advise you to have an abortion," the doctor said as gently as he could.

Rosemary and Louis cried, then talked, then prayed, then cried and prayed some more. "I'm convinced God wants us to have this baby," Rosemary told Louis. "But we are the ones who will have to deal with the disabilities. I honestly don't know if I'm up to it."

It's easy to obey when we want the same thing God wants. The real test of obedience comes when we know that the outcome may not be what we want. Distorted belief tells us that it is risky to obey God. It suggests that we know better than God knows.

A common distorted belief is that if you are obedient, then your life will be great. You can be assured of prosperity, health, and an existence that is generally wonderful. But there is a huge problem with this teaching: What about those Christians who are suffering? What about those great Christians from the past who were tortured, even killed, for their faith? What about the martyred apostles? Are we to assume from their suffering that they were disobedient to God?

Many people today are being manipulated by preachers and teachers who spread such nonsense. For every person who accepts this distorted belief and experiences something positive, there are many others whose faith is laid waste because they are convinced that God is playing favorites—or that he just cannot be pleased.

Regeneration

Denise started attending the church singles group strictly for the social aspects. "There are nice people there," she figured. "I can make some friends—maybe even get a date." But Denise was immediately drawn to the warmth and true friendships she found there. When she came to know the Lord as her personal Savior, her new friends rejoiced with her.

But there were things about Denise that were different from the others in the group, and soon other people were whispering:

"Her language needs some cleaning up," said one.

"Can you believe it?" exclaimed another. "She asked me to go to a *bar* with her!"

"Denise needs to keep her distance from her old friends," a third stated knowingly. "They're pulling her away from her commitment to the Lord."

A common barrier is caused by the distorted belief that

regeneration means a person is instantly transformed into a mature Christian. Many new believers are surprised to find that they face the same struggles and opportunities for sinning as they did before. And many Christians who should know better are quick to condemn others for not being as mature as they think they should be.

The distorted belief barrier keeps us from seeing that regeneration is just what the word says—a new birth. Unless a baby Christian is nurtured, disciplined, and cared for by his or her new family, that person will not be able to grow in the things of God.

This is an especially dangerous barrier, for it causes well-meaning Christians to hurt the vulnerable among us. We understand that it takes time for babies to grow. We make allowances for their mistakes, we pick them up when they fall, we patiently instruct and guide them. What this barrier does is it keeps us from understanding that Christian maturity, too, is a journey. It, too, takes a person through many different stages of development. For every one of us, old Christians and new, regeneration is a life-long process that will not be completed until we are in heaven.

Peace

Maria's husband and son were flying home from a special father and son celebration when their plane hit the side of a mountain and burst into flames. Grief-stricken and in shock, Maria cried out to the Lord to give her some sense of peace. "You promised you would never leave me or forsake me," she cried out in her pain, "but now when I need you most, you are gone from me. You have left me to bear this all alone!"

Had God left Maria? Of course he hadn't. It's just that in her pain and confusion, the peace she should have gotten from the knowledge that God was right there beside her had run up against a profound blockade. Her heart couldn't feel his presence, so she felt abandoned.

There are going to be times when our hearts will feel abandoned. It is then that we need to overrule our feelings, and through our tears say with hymn writer Horatio Spafford:

"Whatever my lot, Thou hast taught me to say,
'It is well, it is well with my soul!'"

Our experience insists:

- "A God who is all powerful wouldn't let bad things happen."
- "It is my responsibility to see that people are saved."
- "I should be able to simply right my wrongs and be done with it."
- "I can't forgive because that would mean I would have to be reconciled."
- "I should be a mature Christian *right now*."
- "If you were a real Christian, you would be mature *right now*."

We must never allow such arbitrary and emotional influences as our experiences to dictate our beliefs. Our beliefs must always be grounded in one thing and one thing alone— the unchangeable Word of God. Only then will we be able to stand up against barrier #4: our emotional defenses.

Questions for Reflection and Discussion

1. It has been said that "God gave us rules to live by, and that people have been adding to the list ever since." Can you identify some rules that you must live by? How do these affect you? What do they say about God's character? How do they create barriers in your life?

2. Read Isaiah 29:13. How does this Scripture speak of rules creating distorted beliefs which lead people away from God?

3. The Kincaids and the Lambertis shared a friendship and a terrible tragedy: one child lived and the other died. Had the Kincaids experienced more of God's grace because Emily survived? Had they prayed harder? Was their faith stronger? What kind of distorted belief could this kind of thinking generate? What about the Lambertis who lost their little son? Had they not prayed enough? Did they not have enough faith? If they allowed this kind of thinking to continue, what kinds of barriers would be created between them and God?

4. Suzanne's distorted beliefs led her to believe that she must "work off" her sin by helping others. She felt that this payment would ensure her forgiveness. Helping others definitely made her feel better and feeling better about the abortion must mean she was forgiven. What kind of barrier has this belief system created? God has gifts for Suzanne, but her barriers keep her from receiving them. What gifts does he have for her? (Read Ephesians 2:7-8.)

FIVE

▼

BARRIER #4:
EMOTIONAL DEFENSES

William hugged a large heart-shaped rock to his chest. It was uncomfortably heavy, and he struggled to hold it. His jaws tightened and his face reddened as hurt and anger overtook him. With tears welling up in his eyes and his voice quivering, William announced to the small group around him, "This rock is a perfect symbol of my heart."

That's exactly how William saw himself—as cold, hard, and lifeless as an old rock.

William had been taken advantage of in several business deals, and in the process he had lost the gardener's truck and tools with which he made his living. His marriage had already been floundering, and this latest financial disaster pushed it over the edge. His wife had packed up their three young children and moved in with her parents. William was utterly devastated. As far as he was concerned, there was no more life in him than there was in the rock he cradled in his arms.

Shannon had not had a peaceful childhood. Her mother, Louise, still a lovely woman, had been the beauty queen of the Texas town in which she grew up. Right out of high school, Louise had been swept off her feet by the son of a big time rancher. Their wedding was the society event of the year. But after the honeymoon, everything changed. Living on an isolated ranch was far different from being the belle of the town social scene. A nicely appointed parlor was much more Louise's style than a dusty ranch house. And without her constant circle of friends, she had no one to talk to or be with. She found her solace in the bottles in the wine cellar.

For as long as Shannon could remember, her father worked long hours, her mother drank, and she entertained herself. That was their family routine.

Louise was not a pleasant drunk. As the years went on, she became increasingly cruel to Shannon, constantly ridiculing her and criticizing everything she did. At times, the cruelty turned physical, and Louise would beat her daughter severely. Shannon learned early in life that home was not a safe place to be, but there was no where else for her to go.

Throughout her entire life, Shannon stuffed her rage deep down inside herself. She never married; she never even managed to have a real friendship. Now at thirty-eight, she was alone, bitter, depressed, and increasingly crippled with arthritis.

Most of us have experienced trauma and hurt. Some of us, like William and Shannon, have had our hearts and spirits terribly crushed. People who should have been safe and nurturing turned out to be dangerous and untrustworthy. When they should have protected us, they caused us harm.

They left us wounded and confused and bitter and disillusioned.

We all suffer disappointments and pain, but when the anger and bitterness are allowed to establish roots and grow, they can emerge as formidable barriers that destroy us from within.

STOP THE PAIN

Often when we have been badly hurt, especially if it happened when we were young, we are driven to try to make the world less threatening. In an attempt to protect ourselves from further trauma and pain, our hearts raise up defenses. We develop deep calluses around our hearts that keep us from feeling and responding to anything and anyone that might make us hurt—including God.

Read on to see how emotional barriers can affect our understanding of our Heavenly Father.

Holy

When Laura was growing up, her parents made sure she understood that failure would mean misery. Even admitting the wrong didn't stop her mother and father from harping on and on about what had happened. Laura reacted by creating an image of God that wouldn't be a threat to her need to avoid failure at all costs.

For Laura, God only had a "soft" side. She dwelt on his love and goodness and kindness and mercy. She never wanted to consider what "Holy God" meant. She wanted to know nothing at all about his laws or requirements, and certainly not about his judgment. But by limiting God, Laura was never able to see that he meets his own standards, that he is totally trustworthy and consistent.

At forty-one years of age, Laura was diagnosed with cancer of the liver. She was devastated. How could her good, kind, loving Father-God let this happen to her? He was supposed to take care of her! He was supposed to protect her from bad things. "So," she said, "God is just like my father after all!"

Throughout her life, Laura had done her best, but she had failed to reach the impossible standard of behavior she had set for herself. Not just once, but again and again. Never having understood God's holiness, she was convinced that the cancer was God's punishment to her for her failures.

Our need to defend our picture of the God we have created in our minds is the cause of this emotional barrier. Our definition of "Holy God" is a God that fits our own particular picture, and our barrier was raised to protect that picture at all costs.

There are also other ways we attempt to protect our false idea of God. Convinced that a good Christian should have all the answers, we try to ease the pain of others with pat platitudes and easy scriptural explanations. Several people who knew Laura's situation jumped into this "fix-it" mode. They made such pronouncements as:

- "You will come though this a better person."

- "Trust God and everything will work out fine."

- "Prayer changes things, you know. You must not be praying hard enough."

- "When you learn the lesson God has for you, he won't have to keep teaching you."

- "God won't give you more than you can bear."

- "Be thankful in all things."

The fact of the matter is, there are times when, search as we may, we just are not able to find satisfactory answers. When that happens, our emotional defenses scream out: *I knew it! God's credibility is damaged!* or *See? When I need God, he isn't there for me!*

Unanswered questions are not comfortable. But they only challenge the holiness of God when our emotional defense barriers trip us up.

Grace

"I'm not a bad person!" Steve protests. "I mean, I'm not perfect, but I can make my own way."

Steve has a major emotional defense barrier that is barring him from experiencing God's grace. It takes a heartfelt understanding of grace to really own our failures. We don't embrace the darkness of our souls because we cannot admit to our failure, or to the devastation it has caused in our lives. A person who won't admit failure cannot know God's grace.

Think of it this way: Suppose Steve takes an early evening ocean swim. He starts out relaxed and enthusiastic, but then he begins to grow tired. His muscles cramp and his breathing grows labored, but the beach is still a long way off. As he feels his strength ebbing, a voice calls out, "Are you in trouble?"

Rather than admit to his exhaustion, Steve replies as calmly as he can, "No, I'm fine."

As he strains and gasps, the voice calls out again, "Are you sure you don't need help?"

As firmly as he can, Steve replies, "No, I'll be all right."

Sounds pretty foolish, doesn't it? In fact, it sounds more than foolish—it sounds ridiculously disastrous. Yet this is exactly what Steve is saying to God: "No, thank you, God. I can handle this myself!"

Our emotional defenses build up a barrier of pride that we believe—mistakenly—will keep us from being weak and dependent.

Justification

Kimberly spent so much time in the rest room at work that she found it increasingly difficult to hold down even a part time job. First it was just washing her hands over and over, then it was scrubbing her face and arms. Finally it was bathing and showering again and again.

"Why?" her perplexed mother asked.

"Because I'm dirty!" Kimberly answered. "I'm always dirty!"

For years, Kimberly had been sexually abused by first her father and then her uncle. Now, as a young adult, she was still trying to make the all-encompassing "filthiness" go away.

So often, that is exactly what our emotional defenses cry out to us: "You're not *really* justified. Keep washing! Do it again—and again—and again. You are still not clean enough." This emotional barrier causes us to question not only God's love, but also his power to truly change our lives.

I have talked to many people who are convinced they have fallen too far, they have failed too miserably, for even God to change them. I usually ask such a person a question we would all do well to consider: "Are you telling me that the God who created the universe with a word of command can't handle the mess you have made out of your life?"

Sin

Many of us become obsessed with thinking about sin. It is a concept terribly entangled with culture, with church teaching, and with personal experience. To the missionaries who went to the Polynesian islands in the 1800s, it was a sin for the islanders to be less than fully dressed. Their insistence that everyone wear European-type clothing caused a great deal of resentment and resistance to the gospel. Was the native dress really sinful?

To Glenna's mother, to be "lazy" was a sin—lazy meaning not being constructively occupied every minute of the day. Should she catch Glenna "wasting time" reading or drawing or fixing her hair, she would admonish, "Lazy hands are the devil's workshop!"

For Wayne, any use of alcohol was a sin. He refused to believe that Jesus did, indeed, turn water into wine. "If it was wine," he insisted to his questioning neighbor, "it was only because the juice had been sitting out in the sun too long!"

The only sex education Lynn ever got were the whispered admonitions to never, ever be like those "bad girls" who would satisfy boys' disgustingly sinful desires. When she tried to ask her mother a few hesitating questions, she was told, "Shame on you for having such a dirty mind!"

Guess what? Glenna cannot sit down to read a book without feeling great guilt over her laziness. Wayne has just changed churches because of his outrage at seeing the daughter of a prominent church member toasted with champagne at her wedding. And Lynn is getting a divorce; she never was able to get past her revulsion at her husband's desire for a sexual relationship.

Obviously, we need to be concerned about sin taking root in our lives. However, it is also essential that we be sensitive to the Holy Spirit as he leads us into dealing with our sin. No person has ever become better by thinking about sin obsessively or compulsively. The flesh—that is, our natural abilities—cannot overcome the evil embedded within us. The moment we think we have straightened ourselves out, pride and intolerance for others are sure to jump right in and take over.

Forgiveness

When sixteen-year-old Jennifer tearfully told her parents she was pregnant, they quickly arranged for her to go stay with her aunt in another state and have an abortion. "That way no one will have to know," her mother told her. "Everything will be fine."

When Jennifer got back home, her mother greeted her with, "See? It's all over now. No one will ever have to know."

But it wasn't over for Jennifer. She knew.

When Jennifer asked her parents to go with her to talk to their minister about what had happened, they exclaimed, "Whatever for? That's all over and done with. You made a mistake. Now just put it behind you and get on with your life!"

So Jennifer went to the minister alone. To her amazement, he wasn't horrified by what she said. He didn't condemn her or tell her how sinful she was. What he did do was ask her if she had asked God for forgiveness.

"Oh, yes!" Jennifer said. "Again and again and again!" Then, bursting into tears she exclaimed, "But it's such a *big* sin! It's not like just lying or cheating on a test or taking money from my mother's purse. It's a *really big* sin!"

Our emotions tell us that some sins are forgivable, others are borderline, and some are just too great for God to forgive. For those huge sins we will have to pay, and pay big time. Although we might not state it in these words, this barrier separates out certain sins and labels them "unpardonable."

Obedience

I'll never forget the Sunday School offering envelopes of my childhood. Each week we would take an envelope, put our money inside, lick the envelope to seal it, than we would check off the appropriate boxes on the back:

Attending Sunday School	10 points
Brought Bible	20 points
Read Lesson	20 points
Memorized Bible Verse	20 points
Staying for Worship Service	20 points
Put Offering Inside	10 points

Then we added up our scores, which were transferred onto a big chart on the wall of our Sunday School room. The child who got the highest score got a gold star and special surprise.

Now, I wasn't adverse to stretching the truth on my envelope—many an unread lesson was checked off as read. Even so, I never achieved the status of "prize-winning Christian."

I can't remember much about the lessons from my Sunday School days, few of the assigned memory verses stuck with me, and I can't recall a single one of the songs we sang. But one message remained indelibly imprinted on my mind for years: "You are not that great a Christian, kid!"

It's hard to obey when you are certain you'll always come up short.

Regeneration

Randy had a quick temper, and when he was angry, his language turned foul enough to embarrass the saltiest of sailors. Over and over, his wife Nancy complained about his embarrassing outbursts.

"Well," he would say, "that's just the way I am. That's how my father is, it's how my brother is, and it's how I've always been."

"But your father and brother aren't Christians," Nancy would say. "You are!"

"Maybe so," Randy answered, "but a person just doesn't change the habits of a lifetime."

Emotional defense barriers insist, "That's just the way I am. I can't help it, so don't expect me to change." These barriers do two things: First, they deny the power of God to remake us. Second, they remove from us any sense of responsibility for our behavior.

No, we don't necessarily change overnight. But with the barrier down, we *do* change.

Peace

Gene could not get over what had happened. Two years earlier he had lost his wife Tracy as she was about to deliver their first child. Something had unexpectedly gone wrong, and both mother and baby died.

"Peace?" Gene demanded sarcastically. "My wife and baby are gone! There is no peace for me."

Patty, on the other hand, would be quick to describe herself as at peace. Her family and friends would agree. She always seemed happy and seldom complained, even though her family made fun of her overweight body.

Ridicule was something with which Patty was well acquainted. All the time she was growing up, kids had made cruel jokes and rhymes about "fatty Patty." But she was always a good sport about it, laughing through her hurt feelings. She wasn't about to let anyone know how much it pained her.

When Patty was fourteen, her parents took her brother and sister to a dude ranch for vacation, but they sent Patty to a "fat camp." Although she was humiliated and felt left out, she acted as though it didn't bother her at all.

When at twenty-four Patty married Anthony, she felt lucky to have gotten a husband. From day one, Anthony was in charge. He handled the money and gave her an allowance, and she was expected to account for every penny she spent. Each morning before he left for work, Anthony would present Patty with a list of her responsibilities for the day. She was instructed to check each one off as she completed it, and then the fully marked list was to be presented to him when he came home in the evening. Patty's opinion was never asked on anything, and she never offered it.

Patty had long suffered from stomach problems. When her discomfort finally became so severe that she had to seek medical attention, a large stomach ulcer was discovered.

"How is everything at home?" her doctor asked.

"Fine," Patty said cheerfully. "Everything is just fine. I get along well with everyone. I never get upset or angry."

Gene's emotional defense barrier says, "You cannot have peace as long as you are feeling pain." Patty's emotional defense barrier declares, "If you deny your angry feelings, you are at peace. You may have ulcers, but you *are at peace*."

Our emotional defenses tell us:

- "I must protect God's reputation."
- "Hey, I am the victim here!"
- "I'm a bad person, and I can't change."
- "I never get angry."
- "I'm too angry to have peace."

Emotional defenses can protect us from being hurt. But when they become barriers, they can bar God's power from our lives.

"But," you may say, "I have to have some control over my life!"

Good point. And that is exactly what we will be discussing in chapter 6.

Questions for Reflection and Discussion

1. William's heart had become as hard as the stone he held; the pain had been overwhelming, and something had died within him. When people met him, they encountered his coldness and indifference. Nothing seemed to matter to him anymore. His pain had created an impenetrable barrier that would let nothing inside, not even God. His barriers protected him from the possibility of more hurt and they served him well. After all, a "dead" person cannot be hurt.

   Can you identify with William? Have you ever felt dead emotionally? Pray and ask God to show you the messages which hold the "bricks" of emotional deadness in place. What do these "bricks" tell you about God's character? How do they build such a powerful wall, a barrier between you and God? What would God want to say to you about this wall?

2. Think of the times when you have felt crushed by another, when your heart has been wounded. Ask God to

show you the barriers that might have been created in these times of emotional pain.

3. How can we create an emotionally "safe" God of our own making? Reflect back to Laura's story. She created a God who was absolutely not like her natural father, and that made God safe. How does this nice view of God create barriers?

4. Remember the story about Steve, who went out for a swim and ended up in trouble—but his pride wouldn't let him admit he needed help? His pride wouldn't allow him to be vulnerable. How does pride create an emotional barrier between us and God? Is it easier for you to give than receive? How are you doing in the pride, vulnerability, and humility areas?

SIX

BARRIER #5: CONTROL

No sooner would Joel and Christine back their car out of the driveway than, invariably, an argument would start. It didn't matter whether the trip was to the grocery store two blocks away, or a month-long, cross-country vacation.

"There's a stop sign," Christine would announce as they approached the first corner.

"I know there's a stop sign!" Joel would snap. "I'm not blind!"

A bit later Christine would say, "You're awfully close to the car ahead."

"I'm fine!" Joel would shoot back.

"Not if they stop fast, you aren't," Christine would answer. "You've got to have a car length between you for every ten miles per hour you're going."

"That's ridiculous. Two car lengths and someone zips in no matter how fast I'm driving."

And so it always goes.

The problem isn't that Joel is a bad driver, nor is it that Christine is a hopeless nag. The problem is that she just cannot relax when he is at the wheel. She sits stiffly upright, telling him when to go, when to stop, when to slow down, when to speed up, where to turn—and should he make a mistake along the way, you can be sure she is ready to point it out. The carpet on the passenger side of their car is actually worn through from where she stomps on the "brake." Driving with Christine leaves Joel angry and resentful, and it leaves her a nervous wreck. They both hate their time in the car together.

That's pretty much how it is in many of our spiritual lives. We turn ourselves over to God and tell him, "The wheel is yours. You take over. I'll go wherever you want me to go." But as soon as he takes the wheel, we cry out, "No, no. Don't take me there. Turn here! Go that direction!" We stomp on the brake and say, "Stop! This is the wrong way! Go back!"

For many of us, this final barrier is the most formidable of all: We simply cannot stand not being in control. We erect control barriers in an effort to create order and a sense of predictability in our lives. If we can manage our relationships, we believe we can control our destinies.

In Juanita's house, everything was always in perfect order. No glasses were left on the kitchen counter, no papers lay on the coffee table, no fingerprints marked the windows. Juanita spent hours each day cleaning and recleaning, washing and rewashing, straightening and restraightening. Although everything looked perfect, she was constantly irritated with her children and her husband Bert who, she claimed, were all hopeless slobs.

Bert couldn't understand his wife's growing compulsion

for cleanliness. She had always been neat and attractive, but this was ridiculous. The lovely young girl he had fallen for was turning into a nagging shrew.

As the children grew older, they spent more and more time playing at their friends' houses, and Bert spent more and more time at work. Juanita was hurt, but she just couldn't back off her cleaning frenzy.

Twenty years before, to the shock and horror of her family, Juanita and Bert had had to get married when she discovered she was pregnant. Juanita loved Bert, and she couldn't be more proud of her two children, yet she could not cease her frantic compulsion to "be clean." What she couldn't see was that her obsession with her house was an effort to gain control of her own feelings of inner filthiness.

Clark, too, struggled with a control barrier.

Clark was desperately in love with his beautiful wife Stephanie; she meant everything to him. And he was so proud of her for having conquered a teenage drinking problem. When he found the first liquor bottle in the trash, he asked her what was going on. "I've been under a lot of stress lately," she explained, "but I'm working it out. Just be patient with me."

Clark was patient, but Stephanie's drinking increased. For ten years Clark had been in the ministry, and the church was thriving under his leadership. He was happy and fulfilled. But what if Stephanie's drinking were to be discovered? The church would figure that if he couldn't control what was happening in his own family, he certainly wouldn't be able to control an entire church. His ministry could be over.

Clark's solution was to hide the problem. He covered for

Stephanie when she forgot to pick the kids up from school. He made up reasons why she should not be expected to attend church meetings and school functions. Whenever she did have responsibilities, Clark was always careful to have a back-up plan in case she didn't follow through. All the time Stephanie's problem was growing, yet Clark's pride, and his fear of being discovered, kept him struggling to keep up the appearance of normalcy.

Clark was in the middle of a staff meeting at church when the police called. Stephanie had been arrested and charged with drunk driving. The secret was out.

A control barrier says: "You must take care of everything. You are responsible for everyone." By its very actions, it insists: "You can do a better job than God can."

Control barriers are especially dangerous because they require that we trust ourselves more than we trust God. Let's see how control barriers affect the eight concepts we have been considering.

Holy

Therefore God exalted him [Jesus] to the highest place and gave him the name that is above every name, that at the name of Jesus every knee should bow, in heaven and on earth and under the earth, and every tongue confess that Jesus Christ is Lord, to the glory of God the Father.

PHILIPPIANS 2:9-11

If we allow ourselves to have a heartfelt understanding of God and his holiness, we can do nothing but submit to him and to his authority. This is precisely the reason many people do not meditate on his holiness.

When Mario was called into his boss's office, he thought, *What have I done now?* But his boss didn't scold him. On the contrary; he needed a favor. "We just need a few minor changes in the accounting books," the boss said. "See, what happened was, some careless mistakes were made that put us at risk." When Mario didn't answer, his boss' tone changed: "Hey, we're talking about team work here, Mario. You can right the wrong that's been done to us. You can be the hero here or... or you can find another job."

What's wrong with compromising a bit in order to get ahead? Our society makes a big deal over the "self-made" man or woman. But there is a huge problem with a self-made person—the head is invariably too big! Jesus told his disciples that it is easier for a camel to go through the eye of a needle than for a rich man to enter the kingdom of God—in other words, it is not humanly possible. Why? Because a rich man doesn't see his need for God. He figures he can take care of himself.

We don't have to be rich to have this self-sufficiency problem. Any of us who fail to see God in his awesome holiness will try to live life on our own. And not a one of us can do it. It is humanly impossible.

Grace

Relating to God requires that we recognize who he is—including his authority. Our human nature tells us we will be more secure if we stay in control of our lives. Now, here is a real dilemma. On the one hand we have experienced failure and we desperately need to know God's grace. But on the other hand, in order to experience his grace we must give up control.

This leads many Christians to pretend they have received God's grace while proceeding to work themselves senseless trying to overcome the sin in their lives. They know all the right words and all the right motions, so on the surface they may well seem to have it all together. They look askance on those who are struggling and shake their heads righteously at those who are openly failing. "The Christian experience is really so simple!" they proclaim. Yet, within the hidden places of their souls, they struggle on their own against their unseen sins. They major on the externals and ignore the internals.

Elise was such a person. An absolute control freak, everything she did was as close to perfect as it could be. All the time she was growing up, other mothers would point her out to their daughters and say, "Just look at what a good job Elise did! Why can't you be more like her?" As an adult, she had the admiration of everyone around her. What nobody saw was Elise's dependence on prescription pain killers. From the outside, Elise was near perfect. On the inside, she was pained and overwhelmed with condemnation over her failures.

Justification

Russ could hardly contain himself when the pastor told him, "Now that you have accepted Jesus, he has forgiven all your sins. They are gone forever." Two years later, Russ was still praying: "Dear Lord, I know that I am a dirty, rotten sinner. There is nothing about me that is any good at all."

What happened? Russ was a sinner who accepted Christ. Christ took away his sins, declared him righteous, and the Holy Spirit came to dwell in him. So how dare Russ continue to declare himself a dirty, rotten sinner? Doesn't Christ's cleansing work mean anything?

The problem here is that it is easy for us to accept that God has forgiven our sins, but it is not so easy to embrace the fact that we have been declared righteous. Sometimes when I (Robert) am speaking before a roomful of people, I say, "Assuming that everyone here has accepted Jesus Christ as Savior and Lord, tell someone else in the group here: 'Because of Jesus, you have been justified and you are as righteous as Christ.'" Then I tell them to turn to that same person and say, "Because of Jesus, *I* have been justified and *I* am as righteous as Christ." Then I ask them, "Which declaration can you most easily accept as true?"

Without exception, people answer, "The first!"

The frequency with which we see this barrier isn't surprising when we seem to have such a need to produce our own righteousness that we can hardly accept righteousness from God.

Sin

Bruce was a respected elder in his church, and he had been for thirteen years. People looked up to him with admiration and respect. He was considered a perfect family man with a perfect job who led a perfect life. No one would ever have guessed that Bruce waged a constant battle with pornography.

Actually, Bruce had been waging his battle since the age of fifteen. Over and over again he had begged God to take the desire from him. He pleaded with God to give him the strength to get rid of his "collection," or at least to stop adding to it. He hated himself for what he was doing. He hated the sneaking around, he hated the sleazy shops, he hated living in fear that he would be found out.

What Bruce hated most was the complete control his sin held over him.

The control barrier of sin is indeed a formidable one. Our sin nature sets us up for constant conflict between the flesh and the Spirit, and it tells us that we can win the fight by ourselves. It insists we can deal with the sin in our own strength. While Bruce hated having to sneak around and worrying about getting caught, he unfortunately did not hate the sin itself. He weighed the hatred for his behavior against its "benefits," and he decided he was not ready to give up the pornography.

"What can I do?" Bruce asked me. "I've prayed and prayed that God would take away this desire and make me stop, but so far he hasn't."

"Perhaps it's time to change your prayer," I suggested. "Why not specifically give God permission to convict you of the evil of your sin?"

This kind of prayer allows us to see that we are responsible for the sin, and it leads us to godly sorrow and true repentance. This kind of prayer releases our control grip by acknowledging that we cannot heal ourselves.

Forgiveness

Todd sinned. In accordance with the Matthew 18:15-17 guidelines for dealing with a brother or sister in sin, he had been confronted by Max and Reuben, two Christian brothers from church. Todd tearfully acknowledged his sin and asked for forgiveness. He also confessed his sin to God.

That was two months ago. Todd is still apologizing and asking Max and Reuben for forgiveness. And he is still pleading with God to forgive him as well.

Why can't Todd accept the forgiveness God has already extended to him? Why can't he let go of the sin that has already been removed as far from him as the east is from the west? Because a control barrier prevents him from releasing his sin into God's forgiving hands, Todd feels driven to do something that will make up for what he did.

Obedience

When Luke's grandparents sent him a generous check for his tenth birthday, Luke announced, "Now I can finally get that BB gun I've been wanting!"

Reluctantly agreeing, Luke's parents made him and his twelve-year-old brother Ryan sit down for a BB gun safety lesson. They laid out strict conditions under which the boys would be allowed to use the gun. Yet the following day, a neighbor informed Luke's parents he had caught the boys using the *For Sale* sign on his front lawn for target practice. The BB gun was taken away and put on the top shelf of the closet, where it was to stay until further notice.

Four days later, Ryan could stand the restriction no longer. Carefully he took his brother's gun down, tucked it under his jacket, and carried it to the back yard. No one else was home, so who would know? And anyway, what difference could it make?

Ryan fired at a couple of rocks in the yard, then at a lizard that was unlucky enough to slither by. But when Ryan looked up, he was startled to see Luke staring down at him through the kitchen window.

"I'm telling on you!" Luke called. "You're going to be in big trouble!"

"Keep your mouth shut!" Ryan called back. Then he came up with a bright idea; he'd scare his little brother. He emptied the BBs out of the gun, then, assuming his most threatening expression, he aimed the gun at Luke and pulled the trigger. To his horrified amazement, he heard a BB ping inside the "empty" gun. Then he heard an even more horrifying sound—the shattering glass of the kitchen window.

Why had Ryan done such a foolish thing? He wasn't a bad boy, certainly not violent. "I don't know why I did it," he told his parents. "I just wanted to use the gun, that's all."

The very idea of obedience throws a barrier before us. We don't like to obey! If we have to obey, we have to give up control. This control barrier tell us: "Don't let anyone tell you what to do! Be your own person. Do your own thing. Hey, what can happen?"

Regeneration

"Be all you can be!"

"Make yourself over into a new person!"

"Your future is in your hands!"
"Nothing is too hard for you!"
"You can do anything if you try!"

We read these admonitions in books, see them touted on videos, and hear them expounded in countless seminars. Good motivational one-liners, right? Well, yes, to a degree. While it is certainly healthy to work toward achieving all the potential God created in us, taken to the extreme this personal motivation creates a serious barrier. The emotional regeneration barrier tells us that we can remake ourselves into whatever we want to be. It tells us we can control who and what we are. It says we don't need Christ to do the work of regeneration. It insists we can save ourselves.

Peace

Connie and Greg had a great family, as they always knew they would. They'd had it all planned since they married at twenty-one. Greg finished college so he could get a good job, which he did, and Connie had three children, which she and Greg had planned. Rachel was the oldest, Erin came along three years later (that's what all the books said was the best age difference between siblings), and little Seth was born three years to the month later.

Each school year, Connie and Greg selected the teachers their children would have. They choreographed the kids' lives with a well-balanced slate of lessons, sports, enrichment options, and church activities. That's not all: every Monday evening was designated "family night." They spent the time together, entertaining and enjoying one another, then ending with a time of Bible study and family prayer.

The order and control Connie and Greg maintained over their lives provided them with peace and assurance. What they couldn't see was that it created a pervasive tension in the children. There was no spontaneity, no freedom of choice, no opportunity for decision making—and absolutely no room for mistakes.

Connie and Greg were so proud of their family that they let no opportunity to show the kids off—or to offer a word of advice to less fortunate families—slip by them.

The children are now all in their twenties. Connie and Greg still love them dearly, but they don't show them off any more. Rachel got pregnant at sixteen, married at seventeen, divorced at eighteen, and had a second child at twenty. She and her children now live with Connie and Greg. Erin went away to school, and her parents seldom see or hear from her anymore. They know next to nothing about her life. Seth is at home and attending junior college, but his parents have caught him using drugs, and they are worried about his alcohol consumption.

Although we find it hard to accept, control bars us from experiencing peace. The harder we try to control, the less likely we are to succeed. "Taking care of business" can become so distorted that we begin to trust ourselves more than we trust God. Like Connie and Greg, we may *feel* in control, but it is just an illusion.

Not only do control barriers affect us, they affect those around us. Control defenses tell us:

- "Man created his problems, and he will solve them".

- "I'm not really all *that* guilty".

- "I can be whatever I want to be".

- "I'm in charge of my family".

- "I'm in charge of my life".

In the end, control is simply a question of how we view God's character. He asks, "Will you trust me?" Either we answer, "No," and struggle to retain our place in the driver's seat, or we answer, "Yes, I trust you," and give up that cherished spot. If we relinquish control and trust God, we fix our minds on things that can neither be seen nor understood. But in order to do that, we must first be willing to give up the deceptions we cherish.

Questions for Reflection and Discussion

1. Juanita attained a sense of control as she kept her house clean and in perfect order. Order and cleanliness meant she was "good"; life was predictable and safe. Her neat house became a symbol to her of life. Her external control gave her a sense of security internally—or did it? Did she really need God, or could she handle everything herself? She had no clue that a powerful barrier existed between her head and her heart. Can you guess what it was?

2. What do you think this statement means: "If we can manage our relationships, we believe we can control our

destinies"? If we become "professional" relationship managers, how do these behaviors and attitudes transfer to our relationship with God? How does this build barriers?

3. How does the need to "produce our own righteousness" create a barrier between us and God? What are some behaviors that might be warning signs of this problem? How are you doing in this area?

4. How does the control barrier tell us we can win the fight against sin ourselves? Look back at Bruce's struggle with pornography. What barrier is at work here? How does it keep him in bondage and separated from God?

SEVEN

OUR CHERISHED DECEPTIONS

Lauren's experience barrier told her that people who made mistakes were bad, unlovable, and that they deserved to be punished. Nathan's distorted belief barrier kept him in constant fear that he would never be good enough for God. Jennifer's emotional defense barrier shouted that some sins are just too bad to be forgiven. Todd's control barrier wouldn't allow him to accept God's forgiveness. Each of us seems to have a cherished deception to which we cling, an illusion that gives sustenance and added power to our defense barriers.

Take Victoria, for instance. During our counseling sessions, we identified several barriers that blocked her from experiencing God's love. She summed up the problem in one heartbreaking statement: "People like me... just aren't meant to be loved." Victoria could not believe the truth of unconditional love, and the result of this misconception caused great pain and frustration in many areas of her life. Yet she could not seem to let go of her false belief.

If something causes us pain, it is human nature to want to correct the problem and relieve the discomfort. If you get a rock in your shoe, you take the shoe off and get that sharp stone out of there. If you touch a hot burner on the stove, you jerk your hand away. That's how we are; we move away from the pain—unless something prevents us from acting. And this is exactly what our cherished deceptions do. They prevent us from acting by strengthening and reinforcing the barriers between our heads and our hearts. We assume that we are insulating ourselves from our deeper pain by adhering to misconceptions, but in fact both our deceptive beliefs and our internal barriers maintain our inner anguish.

There are six specific deceptions that seem to be especially insidious.

THE LABELING DECEPTION

"I'm just a worrier by nature," Lorraine always said. "I wish I could learn to trust the Lord, but I'm just not the trusting type of person."

Worrier? Not a trusting type of person? Those aren't statements of fact; they are labels. We use labels in an attempt to explain behavior, both other people's and our own. If we can say, "Well, no wonder she's like that. Her father was an alcoholic, you know," or "He never had a father at home so we shouldn't be surprised," or even the ever-popular generic, "It's not my fault; I grew up in a dysfunctional family."

If we can stamp on a label, we can stop looking for any further reason. And that is precisely the danger of this deception. God is much more interested in our discovering the underlying issues that build up barriers than he is in our discovering labels that might excuse them away. Labels isolate us from the real answers. They block our faith, and they prevent us from approaching the One who has the real solutions to life's troubling situations.

When labels are tacked onto us, either by ourselves or by others, we tend to do one of two things: stand and fight, or sit and agree.

If we are the *stand-and-fight* type of person, we will make such proclamations as:

- "How dare you! I never did that!"

- "I did it, but it wasn't my fault."

- "Hey, join the twentieth century, guy! Everyone does that nowadays."

- "Give me a break! I'm not as bad as a lot of people I know."

- "I may not always tell the absolute truth, but I'm not a bald-faced liar like Fred over there!"

If we are the *sit-and-agree* type of person, we will utter such statements as:

- "If that's what they say I am, that's what I must be."

- "I'm sorry. I wish I could do better."

- "I can't help it."

- "Guess God can't do much with 'such a worm as I.'"

When Mike met April in the church choir, they hit it off right away. A whole group made a habit of going out to coffee after choir practice, and Mike and April always went along. Mike enjoyed April's fun-loving wit, and April was touched by Mike's sensitivity. Soon they were making sure they ended up sitting next to each other at the dessert shop table.

"Just because she's a lot of fun," Mike told himself. "Just because he's such a good listener," April reasoned.

One night at choir practice, April didn't seem to be her old fun-loving self. "Want to go someplace and talk?" Mike asked her. "Just the two of us?"

"That would be nice," April said. She was touched that he picked up on her need to be away from the group.

That was the first of many private after-choir-practice talks. "You're really a special friend," April told Mike. "I wish I could talk to my husband the way I can talk to you."

"I wish my wife enjoyed my company like you do," Mike answered earnestly. Then he quickly added, "Not that it's her fault. I realize she is tired, what with the house and the kids and her job and all. But still, I can't help wishing...."

One night April confided her concerns about her marriage. "Every day, we seem to relate to each other less and less," she told Mike as she brushed a tear from her eye. Mike was so touched, he leaned across the table and took her hand in his. They stayed extra long at the coffee shop that night, and when they left, Mike gave April a long hug. Then he kissed her cheek.

From that night on, the relationship grew until it was a red-hot affair. When Mike and April were finally confronted with what had become common knowledge among their choir friends, April stood and fought:

"Don't blame us! Blame our spouses! This wouldn't have happened if either of us was getting our need for love met at home! And who are you to say we're wrong, anyway? God must have meant for us to be together. He let us meet, and he wants us to be happy."

Mike, on the other hand, sat and agreed with those who were confronting him:

"For years I have been an adulterer in my heart," he said softly. "I guess the only difference is that now you all know what I am. I don't deserve either April or my wife. God will never be able to use me again, not after what I've done!"

Both Mike and April ended up divorcing their spouses, and within the year they were married. But before long Mike began to feel misunderstood, and soon April started to feel neglected. The labels of "neglected" and "adulterer" had kept both April and Mike from dealing with their root problems.

SELF-DECEPTION

Doug was a founding member of the church, an elder on the board. He also was addicted to prostitutes. For years no one suspected his "double life." When his wife Helene discovered to her horror that their substantial savings account was all but empty, she confronted Doug. Relieved to finally be rid of the deception, he admitted everything.

"I don't get it," Helene mumbled in shock. "You mean

you visited a prostitute on Saturday night and served communion in church on Sunday? How could you do that?" Actually, it wasn't that hard. Doug could deceive others, and even thought he could deceive God, because he was a master at deceiving himself.

Christians have no excuse for self-deception, for we have been given the Holy Spirit to convict us of the truth. Why, then, are we deceived? There are three main reasons:

- We put our faith in people rather than in God.

- We would rather believe the lie than the truth.

- We put more value on our reason than on God's Word.

Doug had deceived himself into believing that if nobody knew about the sin, it didn't hurt anyone. And if it didn't hurt anyone, what difference did it make?

"But," you may say, "how can I know if I'm being deceived?"

Good question. And it has an even better answer: Ask God. Give him permission to remove the blinders from your eyes and to allow you to see the truth. Ask him to help you make the right choices as you face the issues before you. Trust him to give you the strength and wisdom to walk honestly before him.

THE RIGHT BEHAVIOR DECEPTION

"Thank goodness I'm not like April or Mike or Doug," you may be saying. "How can they not see the sin in their lives? I can assure you I'm nothing like them. I may not be perfect, but I do act like a Christian."

Really? Always? In all circumstances? Whether you feel like it or not? Even in the privacy of your own thoughts?

Be careful. People who live by the deception that acting right makes you right risk putting their focus in the wrong place.

Over the years, we have counseled many leaders who were burned out in their ministries. They all said some variation of the same thing: "I have consistently done what I really thought was right. So why has this happened to me? Why do I feel so empty inside? If I've done it right, how can it turn out wrong?"

Of course obedience to the Lord is important. Certainly there is a degree to which our deeds demonstrate our faith. The problem lies with our inner motivations.

Jesse was a minister who burned out doing good. "All I could think about was getting the job done," he recalls. "If you had asked me back then, 'Why are you working non-stop?' I would have said, 'Why? I'm doing it for God, of course!' And I really would have meant it. But when I look back on it now, I know it was *my* goals I was intent on meeting. It was *my* success that was on the line."

If we were to be brutally honest about it, most of us would have to admit that we are trapped in a greater need for approval from man than from God. What most of us think we are doing for the kingdom of God, we are actually doing for other people. The distinction is hard to see because our heart motivation gets clouded by the "right behavior" rules in which we so heartily believe.

Regardless of how it looks from the outside, our ministries will only be meaningful if our actions are God-motivated. Our accomplishments will only be significant if we bring God into each situation. We will only be successful if we minister in his wisdom and strength.

THE IGNORANCE-IS-BLISS DECEPTION

When I was growing up, I (Rujon) was taught not to question what I was told. In school, we memorized facts and we were tested on how accurately we repeated them back. There was much more emphasis put on facts than on critical thinking and analysis.

This is certainly how it was for Philip. He did well in school, he got good grades, and he didn't debate with anyone in authority. In a graduate class at Fuller Seminary, Philip was asked to explore Christianity through the eyes of American popular culture, focusing particularly on television and movies and how they reflected the values of our society.

Philip sat down to write his paper, but he had no clue where to begin. "How did those messages impact me as a Christian?" he recalls. "I hadn't the faintest idea. I'd never been taught to think critically, or to really analyze material. Throughout my elementary, high school, and college years I had done little more than take the data and report it back in the way my teachers wanted to hear it. The method worked well. I graduated from a well-respected university with honors."

For the first time, Philip realized this was the same way

he had always approached his Christianity. He didn't question it, or even think about it too much. He just believed what he was told.

The danger of this "don't ask" approach to Christianity is that it leaves us in the "arrival zone" of knowing God where we can easily fall prey to deceptions. There is nothing wrong with asking questions. If we don't believe God's Word can stand up under scrutiny, then we *really* have problems. The fact is, the process of thoughtful study and meditation does result in tough questions. But then, finding God's answers creates "tough" Christians, for after asking and pleading and searching and pondering, we emerge on the other side knowing the One in whom we believe.

God wants us to know him in a way that moves beyond mere facts. He is not bothered by our hard questions. His desire for us is a real relationship with us that extends from his heart to ours.

THE LEARNING LIMITATION DECEPTION

Dr. Ed Young, pastor of the Second Baptist Church of Houston, Texas—one of the largest churches in America—aims to reach as many people as possible. Never one to fear trying new things, he is innovative and creative, and his sermons are effective.

One Sunday Dr. Young gave a bracelet to each member of the congregation. During the sermon, he referred to the bracelet beads one by one, each of which illustrated a specific point. People could *see* the message, they could *touch* the message, they could *interact* with the message. Several hundred people accepted Christ that day. One woman said it for all: "I've been in church hundreds of times, but today, for the first time, I saw and felt and really experienced the sermon."

Dr. Young was willing to break away from the typical method of sermon delivery, but it could never have been successful unless the congregation was also willing to break out of its accustomed style of learning. This is one church that refuses to be deceived by learning limitations. They accepted Dr. Young's challenge to do something different.

THE HUMANISTIC CHRISTIANITY DECEPTION

Carla was full of questions. Her strained credit card attested to the enormous amount she spent on Christian books, tapes, videos, and workbooks. She had seen more counselors than she could keep track of. Now she was coming to me (Rujon) for answers.

After thirty minutes, it became clear that my answers were not bringing the satisfaction Carla was hoping for. "Why can't anyone give me a simple answer?" she cried in frustration. "What about all the people in the world who don't have Christian bookstores where they can buy the tapes and books and things? Does God teach them himself? Can't he teach me?"

Actually, if God himself were to sit down and talk to Carla, I'm not so sure she would accept his answers, either. If he were to say, "Trust me," she might well say, "Why?"

That's because she didn't really want difficult spiritual answers. She wanted easy human answers. Carla was being deceived by humanistic Christianity.

The danger of the humanistic approach to life is that it accepts man as the final discoverer and determiner of truth. Man the creation becomes dependent upon himself rather than upon God the Creator.

In our heads we know that the Holy Spirit can teach and guide us, but our hearts won't accept it. Language barriers arise to shout, "It doesn't compute!" Experience barriers scream, "I can't trust God!" Distorted belief barriers insist, "That's not the way I believe!" Emotional barriers cry out, "It doesn't feel right!" Control barriers insist, "I can do it!"

THE PROBLEM WITH DECEPTIONS

As we said at the beginning of this chapter, deceptions are insidious. We can be caught in their grasp without even being aware they are out there. If we are convinced we cannot be deceived, then deception is almost certain, for none of us is immune. The only way to prevent being ensnared by deceptions is to make absolutely certain that our foundation is secure.

Questions for Reflection and Discussion

1. Lorraine defined herself with the following label, "I'm just a worrier by nature." What kind of labels have you

defined yourself with? Do these "protect" you in any way? If so, how? What "new" label would God give you? Could you give yourself permission to receive such a gift? If not, why? If yes, then go ahead. Make this a matter of prayer! How would accepting this new "identity" impact your life and relationship with God?

2. Mike and April's relationship gives two excellent examples of how labels are used for protection. How do you see the examples of "stand and fight" and "sit and agree" at work in our story? What does this tell you about how Michael and April were trapped in the deception of labeling?

3. How can we become masters at deceiving ourselves? Try to think of the process and how it unfolds. What are the "rules" for this process to occur? If you can identify them, you will be in a much stronger position to know when they are at work in your life!

4. How does the deception of right behavior create a formula-driven relationship with God? In other words, "If I do this..., then God will do that...."

5. "Ignorance is bliss" is a deception which runs off two powerful engines: denial and ignorance. Try to think of several situations where you have used denial or ignorance for "protection." How do these deceptions lull you into a sense of security? What happened when they didn't work anymore? Read 2 Corinthians 4:6. What does this tell you about God's faithfulness to help you see the "light"?

6. What kind of learner are you? Finding new styles might be a bit frightening. A new style might mean that God will surprise you! Try to think of ways certain learning styles have kept you trapped.

EIGHT

PUTTING DOWN A SOUND FOUNDATION

I (Rujon) was restless, frustrated with the pace of our ministry. It wasn't that I wasn't working hard—I was. And it truly seemed to me that I was doing everything I needed to be doing. I felt I knew the way forward, but had lost my passion. I had worked too hard to make things happen. I was tired and burned out.

One morning in early May my husband suggested that we walk to a nearby coffee shop and treat ourselves to coffee and doughnuts. Sitting on the benches outside, we tossed crumbs on the ground and enjoyed watching the birds scramble for them.

"Look at that one!" my husband exclaimed, pointing to a beautifully colored bird among the flock of little sparrows. But before I could get a good look at it, the bird flew off. I didn't think any more about him until I took the coffee cups back into the shop. The bird had flown inside and was flapping its wings. In its frantic search for a way out, it had come up against a large picture window. Again and again the bird smacked into the glass in a vain attempt to regain its freedom. I knew that unless that bird was rescued quickly, it would surely perish.

I walked over and tried to scoop the wild bird up gently, but it would have no part of me. Only when the bird's strength was so depleted it could no longer resist was I finally able to pick it up and carry it outside to safety. With a sense of satisfaction we watched that beautiful creature soar off into the sky.

"You know," I said to my husband, "I have been a lot like that bird. The way looks so clear to me, and I am so certain I can make it on my own. But like that bird, I've just been hitting a glass window. What I need to do is relax and stay still long enough for God to show me the way."

My "glass window" was an old internal barrier that blocked my way: "You should...," "You have to...," "You really ought to...," "You must...," with the haunting counterpart, "No matter what you do, it won't be enough."

Actually, that last soul cry is right on target. I cannot ever be good enough. Neither can any of us. That's why we need a firm foundation on which to build our lives.

HOW FIRM A FOUNDATION

When Carolyn discovered that her husband Ned was involved in an affair, she was absolutely crushed. She would have left him right then and there had it not been for their three children. But Carolyn knew what it was like to grow up without a father, and long ago she had vowed it would never happen to her kids.

"I'm so sorry," Ned told her. "I don't know what came over me. I really do love you. All I can do is beg you to forgive me."

Carolyn was not at all sure that was possible. She went to see the Reverend Ogden, her pastor. "Ned says he's sorry and he wants me to forgive him," she cried. "He insists he still loves me. He *is* a good father, and before this, I would have said we had a good marriage. But now everything has changed. How can I ever forgive him for what he has done?"

"Forgiveness is God's way," the pastor reminded her.

"But I don't feel the least bit forgiving!" Carolyn insisted.

"You don't have to feel forgiving," he said. "In God's power, you can forgive Ned regardless of your feelings. It's even possible for you to come to the place where you love him again."

For several minutes Carolyn sat in silence, sick at heart. "Why do *I* have to do the forgiving?" she demanded bitterly. "Why do *I* have to be the one to reach out in love when Ned is the one who did wrong? Where is God in all of this?"

"Ah!" responded her pastor. "That is exactly the right question to ask. For you see, God is right there in the center of the command to love the unlovely and to forgive despite the wrong." He reminded Carolyn of the example set by

God himself: He first loved us when we were more unlovable than we can even imagine. He forgave us when our sin was unbearably horrible.

Then he asked, "Have you experienced God's love and forgiveness in your life?"

"Yes!" Carolyn answered emphatically. "You know I have."

"And Ned? Has he?"

"Yes. Certainly." Carolyn was quiet for a long time before she finally spoke. "God loves both of us even though neither of us deserve it. And he has forgiven us in spite of our actions." Then she said, "I think I know what I need to do, Reverend Ogden. I think I need to ask God to let me see Ned through his eyes."

Outside of the Christian context, this is not a generally accepted way of dealing with such a problem. But God has provided us with a better way. The language of Christianity is a language of love and forgiveness. The experiences, beliefs, and emotions we need to foster are experiences, beliefs, and emotions of love and forgiveness. And true love can only be found through God in Jesus Christ.

The majority of people in this country claim to be Christians. They fully agree with teachings about a God of love. "I try my best to do right by my fellow man," one earnest man said. A college student told me, "I may do little things wrong, like fib now and then, but I never do really bad things, like steal or kill." An elderly woman working in her rose garden stated, "I do my best to spread God's love around by making the world a more beautiful place."

We are good to our fellow men. We never do really bad things. We make the world a better place. By these actions, we try to tell ourselves that we have spiritually arrived. It all sounds good and right, but the fact is, without Jesus the real changes are not there. Even our good spiritual choices do not bring us the new life we seek. John 1:13 tells us that the initiative for new life in Christ comes from God. It is a work of the Holy Spirit (John 3:8). We can do nothing to make it happen besides choosing to accept God's gift of Christ as our Savior.

What does it mean to accept Christ as our Savior? We want to experience God's love, but we can never enter into his presence until we become holy enough—which is completely impossible! How can we be reconciled to God in spite of our sinfulness? How does Jesus' holiness and his death on the cros bridge that unbridgeable gap?

These questions are answered more fully elsewhere, but a good understanding of salvation is built upon certain truths. Here are the foundation stones upon which our faith is built:

Building Stone #1: We need from God something we cannot provide for ourselves. The first building stone is to realize our needy condition, our utterly dependent state. We can do nothing until we first acknowledge that in ourselves we are powerless to do anything.

Building Stone #2: Jesus the Christ, the Son of God, is the only way the gap between sinful people (us) and a holy God can be bridged. Jesus is the sinless sacrificial lamb foretold in the Old Testament, offered up for the sins of the world. He offers to let his death be a substitute for our otherwise inevitable (and because of our sinfulness, deserved) death.

Building Stone #3: Jesus Christ's sacrificial gift can only be a reality in my life or in yours if we decide to make it so. We need to say, "Yes, Jesus, be my Savior." This third building stone, the one for which we are responsible, is the one that can make God's gift of love a reality in your life.

Building Stone #4: In response to the forgiveness God offers us, we are required to reach out and forgive one another. We have God's unfailing help to do so. Daily we want to thank and worship him for his love.

Our foundational faith results in hope and freedom and security. We *can* know the truth and the truth *will* make us free. This truth allows us a wonderfully secure intimacy that goes far beyond the security one human being can give another. Just look at the picture drawn for us in Psalm 139:

> Where can I go from your Spirit?
> Where can I flee from your presence?
> If I go up to the heavens, you are there;
> if I make my bed in the depths, you are there.
> If I rise on the wings of the dawn,
> if I settle on the far side of the sea,
> even there your hand will guide me,
> your right hand will hold me fast.
>
> PSALMS 139:7-10

That's true security!

A FOUNDATION OF POWER

Whoever you are, whatever your abilities or liabilities or disabilities, whatever your strengths or your weaknesses, you can construct a barrier-free mansion on this firm foundation of faith.

Ask God for his guidance. Ask him to show you his truth in a way that will allow you to identify barriers and find the way to freedom. Ask him to help you persist in spite of apparent setbacks. Get ready to experience love, freedom, joy, hope, and peace that you never realized existed.

God loves you! This is the greatest truth of all.

Questions for Reflection and Discussion

1. In the story about the bird, Rujon learned that, like the bird, she had to run out of energy—hit the wall—before she would let herself trust God in this new area of her life. How do you come to the place where you will truly trust God and let him have control of your life? How have these times in your Christian life helped you build a stronger relationship with God?

2. Read over each building stone, one at a time. Try to think of one key word or phrase which summarizes what you have read. Now ask the Lord to help you find one or

two key Scriptures for each of the four building stones. Spend some time meditating upon these. Let God bring new revelation and confidence through his word to you!

NINE

HOW DO I BREAK THOSE BARRIERS DOWN?

Not long ago I (Rujon) met a man I will call Brad. The minister of a large and successful church, Brad attended a seminar at which I was speaking. Afterward he took me aside and asked if we could talk for a few minutes. "I stand in the pulpit every Sunday and preach," Brad told me through his tears. "I tell my congregation about the love and acceptance of God. I know it's true in theory, but the fact is, I have never been able to truly accept that God actually loves me."

"What you're saying," I said, "is that you know God's love in your head, but that it has never had an impact on your heart."

"Exactly," Brad admitted. Then, in a soft voice he added, "For as long as I can remember, I have been convinced that God hates me."

"What?" I asked, not sure I had heard correctly. "Did you say you think God *hates* you?"

Brad nodded. "Let's face it," he said, "I'm a miserable failure. That's all I've ever been."

"But your church is so successful," I exclaimed. "Everyone at this seminar seems to know you, and it's obvious that they all respect you and the work you do. You have accomplished so much!"

Ignoring everything I had said, Brad murmured, "I've let God down."

Brad felt comfortable with "doing." Throughout his life, he had done a lot, and his accomplishments had earned him love and acceptance. Now he was pleading, "I want to experience God's love for myself. Tell me, what should I do to make it happen?"

"Nothing," I said.

"What?" he asked in astonishment.

I reminded him that all his doing and trying to earn God's love were what had caused the barrier between his head knowledge and his heart experience in the first place. "Instead of *doing*, ask God to do it," I said. "Ask him to demonstrate his love and acceptance to you."

Brad went away unconvinced.

Like Brad, you may know what the barriers in your life are. Or you may still be unsure. Either way, you are most likely saying, "Okay, but what now?"

You have two choices. You can either ask God to show you your particular barrier and help you to break it down, or you can leave it in place until your life is so miserable you can no longer ignore it. If you choose the latter, watch out.

In 1986, I (Robert) founded Rapha, a company that provided Christ-centered mental health care. The work we did was excellent, we were biblically based in our therapy, and we were successful far beyond anything I had ever imagined. As I looked around at all that had been accomplished through Rapha, I thought, *I've done a good job here. And it was really easy*! You guessed it. I immediately entered the most difficult years of my entire life. Looking at the situation objectively, I know I'm better off today for having gone through all that pain and difficulty, yet I will have to admit that there is a part of me (a very large part, I'm afraid) that wishes I were still basking in that old uninterrupted success.

The painful fact of life is that we cannot take ourselves to maturity any more than we can add six inches to our height. Every one of us is God's project. Take comfort in this. Yet even a young Christian knows that the process of being made into God's image can be so difficult that we want to run away. With God's help, we begin to see the ugliness inside ourselves. None of us likes to have the dark side of our souls revealed.

Yet if we ask God to give us courage, if we refuse to hide from what he shows us, God can break the barriers down. As they come down, we can experience the fulfillment of God's plans for us. We can know the freedom and joy that is possible with God.

So, now the big question: How do I go about cooperating with God to break those barriers down?

DISMANTLING, PIECE BY PIECE

Fresh-from-college young people are so inspiring. They have all the answers. They can see the way so clearly. They forge ahead fully prepared to save the world. Remember how it felt? Instant maturity.

Unfortunately, instant maturity is not reality. The reality is that we have to climb a distance, then fall down, then pick ourselves up and climb as far as we can before we fall down again. Depending on how we handle our past failures and setbacks, the experiences, teachings, and emotions of life begin to form road-blocks. For most of us, our unsteady climb toward maturity results in plenty of blocked passages.

We would like to suggest a four step plan for barrier destruction:

Step #1: Express Your Feelings to God

Patrick prided himself on his ability to control his emotions, and he looked with disdain on people who could not—or would not—do the same. "I never get angry," he calmly told his frustrated and yelling wife. "I simply choose not to."

As soon as I (Robert) met Patrick, I could sum him up in one word: angry.

Patrick would not admit his anger to anyone, not to his wife, not to God, not even to himself. Although he is extreme, most of us are somewhat like Patrick. It's hard to express our feelings, especially those we think we shouldn't have. And yet the first step to breaking down the barriers is to do exactly that—express your feelings to God. Tell him about your anger, your shame, your embarrassment, your frustration.

"But I shouldn't be angry!" Patrick insisted when I told him about this step.

No? Why not? What happens is that we try to make our response to circumstances be what we think it should be rather than recognizing it for what it is. God's unconditional love and acceptance challenge us to face the reality of our situations. When we are seething with anger, God is there. When we are racked with doubts and disbelief, he is there. When we are overwhelmed with pain and sadness and unrelenting grief, God is there. When our lives are rocked by storms or rattled to the foundation by emotional earthquakes, God is right there waiting patiently to be invited to walk through it with us.

"I would much rather have God take me out of it," you may be saying.

We know. We have often felt the same way. But if he did that, he would prevent us from ever growing and maturing. It wouldn't be fair to us.

But being willing to undergo the process of maturation doesn't mean we have to pretend to like it. Even Job, that great paragon of faith and patience, went through a time of telling God in no uncertain terms just how he felt.

When you tell God your feelings, it is important to do it out loud. Voicing your feelings in words is far different from just thinking them in your mind. It keeps you on track, and allows you to be precise and exact.

I knew that Patrick was on his way to bringing down a major barrier when he sat in my office and haltingly prayed, "God, I am angry. I am angry at my wife for not meeting my emotional needs. I am angry at my kids for not being the people I want them to be—for Anna for arguing with everything I say and making me feel frustrated and out of control, and for Darrin for getting his ear pierced without my permission and embarrassing me by wearing an earring. I am angry at my boss for not recognizing the work hours I put in at home. Not once has he so much as thanked me for all the extra work! And I'm angry at you, God, for the helplessness I seem to always be feeling."

Good for Patrick! He is ready for Step #2.

Step #2: Do a Self-Diagnosis

"Why do you think you feel the way you do about expressing your feelings, especially your anger?" I asked Patrick.

"Because anger is a sin," he said firmly.

"Is it really?" I asked.

"For me it is," he insisted.

"Well, then, tell God your diagnosis," I said.

You are probably thinking, *Hey, wait a minute! Feeling angry isn't a sin*! You're right, of course, but at this point we are not dealing with a correct diagnosis versus an incorrect diagnosis. All we want is a *self-diagnosis.* Tell God what *you think* the reason for your barrier is, and ask him to either confirm it or correct it. He may do this by bringing back to your mind something you read, something you heard, or perhaps something from right here in this book. Or he might remind you of a Scripture passage, or perhaps even the words from a hymn.

You may be wondering, *But what if God doesn't let me know whether or not my diagnosis is right?*

It all comes down to a question of trust. Can you trust God to guide you in this matter? Can you trust him to give you the wisdom you need? Let me tell you one thing: God *is* trustworthy—always and in all things. His character is never a problem. The only real question is whether or not you will put your trust in him.

One Sunday afternoon, Patrick called me on the telephone. "You know what?" he exclaimed. "Even Jesus was angry!" In the morning's sermon, the minister had read the account of Jesus throwing the money changers out of the temple, an account Patrick had heard hundreds of times before. But this time, God had shown him that there is a time and a place for anger, and that there is a proper way of expressing it. Patrick made a diagnosis, then he trusted God to show him its validity. And that is just what God did.

Step #3: Tell God What You Are Doing to Change

"I am a reserved person," Patrick said. "And I have spent my life denying my feelings. I can't change all that overnight."

No, none of us can change the patterns of a lifetime that quickly.

"Tell me," I said, "what are you doing to start the change?"

"Well, instead of saying, 'I'm not angry,' I say, 'I don't *think* I'm angry.' It's not much, but it's a start."

That is exactly what God wants—a start. Step #3 is to look at the changes you have made and, in an audible voice, to tell God what they are. They may seem like awfully tiny steps that don't appear to be moving you very far along, but that's okay.

"But I want to change more than this!" Patrick exclaimed.

If the barriers are not coming down, ask God what is keeping you from further change. And then listen for his guidance.

Step #4: Ask God to Bring the Barriers Down

Now you are ready to finally make the way between your head and your heart barrier-free. Ask God to show you any issues to which you may still be clinging.

I gave Patrick a notebook and suggested he write down every experience he could think of that had left him with these messages:

"God must not hear me because I haven't changed yet."

"I can't change."

"This whole process is hopeless."

He wrote: *Yesterday I punished our son for leaving his bike in the front yard by grounding him for the weekend. I didn't realize until later that would mean he would have to miss pitching at his team's baseball game. My wife told me I acted out of anger, not out of reason, and that she thought I should talk to Darrin and come up with a better punishment. I told her calmly but firmly that I was not angry and I would do no such thing. She wanted to argue, so I left and went to get some work done at the office. It's hard to admit even to myself, but I know she is right. I did punish Darrin out of anger. I've told him a thousand times to put his bike away, and I can't stand looking at that earring in his ear! But I never could admit my anger to my wife, and I certainly can't apologize to Darrin. I just cannot change.*

"Do you mean you, Patrick, can't change, or do you mean that God can't change you?" I asked.

"Well…I'm not sure," Patrick said.

I suggested he write down specific messages that seemed to challenge God's work of regeneration in his life. After a bit of thought he wrote: *God is all powerful. I have asked him to change me, but I'm not changed. So how am I a "new creature" in him?*

"Let's pray together," I suggested, "and you can present this seemingly mixed message to God. Invite him to show you his *true* messages about your new identity in him."

When I next saw Patrick, he excitedly showed me his notebook. "Just look at what God brought to my mind!" he exclaimed. "A whole list of times when I *did* acknowledge my anger, not to mention all kinds of other feelings! I was so busy feeling defeated about what I *didn't* do that I was missing all the progress I was making."

"Great list!" I said. "Now go home and hang it somewhere where you will see it every day. Knowing how far God has brought you will help you to keep on moving ahead."

We can hold tightly to our negative experiences, our distorted beliefs, and our emotional defenses, or we can loosen our grasp and let them go. As long as we cling to the old and familiar, the barriers will remain insurmountable.

"But I can't let go!" you may be saying. "I want to, but I just can't!"

Great. Then this is the perfect opportunity for God to display his majestic power and awesome presence in some unexpected way. Ask him to do it, then step back and prepare to be astounded.

Both the motivation and the ultimate power to overcome barriers comes from the unfailing love of

Christ. Not only is he our Savior, but he is our friend and our healer. He is our ultimate source of overcoming power.

Questions for Reflection and Discussion

1. Psalms 25:4-5 says, "Show me your ways, O Lord, teach me your paths; guide me in your truth and teach me, for you are God my Savior, and my hope is in you all day long." Why is a teachable spirit—a willingness to learn—so important in developing an attitude that wants to do business with God?

2. In order to complete the next steps, you need to pray and ask God to bring a specific barrier to your attention—one that he knows you are now ready to deal with. After he shows you, use this information to work through the following exercises.

   a. Step one is to express your feelings to God. In order to do so, you must know how you feel. This is often not such an easy thing to do. (Remember Patrick's story?) Are you aware of your emotions, or are they still unfamiliar territory to you? What might be holding you back?

   b. Step two requires the ability to be honest with yourself. What might get in your way? What kind of prayer would tell you that you were serious or not-so-serious about taking this step?

c. Step three requires that you evaluate what you have been trying to do to change. Look at your behavior and attitudes. What do they tell you about the process you have been in? How do these need to change? Try to think of specific situations.

d. Step four involves two things: revelation from God, and a sincere desire on your part both to see and to work with the truth he shows you. This step requires prayer and hard work, but helps you begin to experience the freedom you desire.

Step four involves:

- Finding time for prayer, earnestly seeking God in a way that gives him "permission" to begin to break through the barriers which have kept him at a distance.

- Asking him to show you what you must do, practically, to make the necessary changes.

- Most of all, giving him time to speak to you and teach you about his character. At some appointed time, you will find that he has made a "love-deposit" within you; one that you know has truly come from him. This "deposit" is what makes change possible and his truth a reality for your life.

TEN

THE POWER TO OVERCOME

It was going to be a rough trip, and the man was not looking forward to it. Not that it was such a long distance from Jerusalem to Jericho—just seventeen miles, less than a good day's journey. But the steep road wound almost straight downhill, from twenty-five hundred feet above sea level to eight hundred feet below sea level. The switchbacks and hairpin turns that made the steep descent possible wove through rocky, brushy desert country. It was the perfect place for robbers and highwaymen to lie in wait for defenseless travelers such as he.

I'll leave Jerusalem at first dawn, the man decided. *No stops, no delays. By God's grace, I'll make it safely to Jericho before nightfall.*

Early the next morning, as the sun was rising, the man donned a shabby cloak he kept for such trips (he didn't dare look too prosperous), tucked his full money purse well inside his clothes where it would be safest, and set off on the road to Jericho.

He was just rounding a sharp curve when he saw a

hooded man standing in the road in front of him. Immediately he sensed danger. But before he had time to think, two other men jumped from the brush beside the road. The hooded highwayman grabbed his donkey, and the other two pulled him off.

"Where is your money?" one demanded.

When the man insisted he had no money, one robber hit him in the face, sneering, "Never mind! We'll find it!"

The three ripped his cloak off him. Then, punching and kicking him, they pulled off the rest of his clothes, piece by piece. When the money purse finally tumbled out, they cheered, then they fell on him in earnest. Finally one called out, "That's enough! He's as good as dead!" After one final kick in the face, the laughing, jeering robbers led the man's donkey away.

A short time later, a priest traveling down the road came upon the man's crumpled body. "Tsk, tsk," he chortled. "What *is* this world coming to? It's gotten so that a man can't even travel in peace anymore!" And with that he crossed over to the other side of the road. The battered man managed to lift his head just enough to hear the priest utter another "Tsk, tsk, tsk!"

The sun rose high in the sky, punishing the man's bruised and bloody body. He heard someone else approach, but he was too weak to lift his head again.

"Oh, what is this?" the religious man, a Levite, exclaimed when he saw the beaten man. "Ugh! Maybe he's dead! I can't defile myself...." And with that, he, too, crossed over to the other side of the road and hurried on his way.

The man lay unmoving. He desperately wanted to call out for water, but his lips were too swollen and parched to form words. And even if he could have called out, there was no one around to hear his cries. The sun was no longer high in the sky. Soon dusk would come, then cold night would fall. That would be the end.

Then the man heard the sound of approaching hooves. It was someone on a donkey. But this time the man didn't even bother to open his eyes. There was no use.

But what was this? A hand touching his face? Water gently trickling through his lips and onto his tongue? Soothing oil and soft cloths on his wounds?

"Don't worry," a voice said gently. "I'm going to get you up on my donkey. I know you are hurting, but it's not too far to Jericho. When we get there, we'll get you into a real bed. We'll get a doctor, and medicine, and anything else you need to help you be comfortable while you get well."

The man couldn't open his eyes to see his benefactor, but the accent was unmistakable. He was a Samaritan. Normally the man, a Jew, wouldn't allow such a dog of a human being to so much as brush against him, let alone to actually pick him up. And since this Samaritan man knew perfectly well how much he was detested, why would he be putting himself out to get a Jewish stranger safely to Jericho? It didn't make sense. But the man was too weak to try to figure it out—and too grateful for the help to care where it came from.

Although the Samaritan stranger did all he could to ease the man's discomfort, the trip seemed endless. Every little while, the Samaritan would wipe the man's face with a cool, damp cloth, and dab a bit of water on his tongue. He held him gently on the donkey and whispered, "It won't be long now. Just hang on—we'll be there soon."

The man remembered little of that first night in Jericho. What he did remember was that the Samaritan man never left his side, not for a moment. All night long he ministered to the man's needs, faithfully watching over him. Early the next morning, the Samaritan man said, "I have business to attend to, so I will have to leave. But you will be well cared for here, and I'll be back to check on you in a couple of days."

On his way out, the Samaritan man said to the innkeeper, "Look after him. Here's money to pay for his care. If it costs more, spend it. I'll repay you when I get back."

Does this sound familiar? We all know the story of the Good Samaritan. God gives us many opportunities to minister to each other's needs, to be true friends and healers to our brothers and sisters, and he expects us to do so faithfully. We can think of many instances when "good Samaritans" have reached into our lives, and we know we have been able to do the same in the lives of others. But regardless of our desires and motivations, we are too likely to be like the priest or the Levite.

"How sad!" we say, shaking our heads and sighing. "What *is* this world coming to?" Then we gingerly step to the other side, piously saying, "I'll pray for you!"

Other times we are so involved in our own lives that we

just don't see the needs around us. Or it may be that we see and we care, but we just don't know what to do. Or we are repulsed. Or we feel helpless.

JESUS, FRIEND AND HEALER

Jesus gives an entirely new meaning to the word "friend." He promises, "Never will I leave you; never will I forsake you" (Heb 13:5). Not only does he care enough about us to stick beside us no matter what, but he has the power to keep his word and actually *do* it.

To know Jesus as friend is to accept that he knows everything about us—the noble and the horrible, the beautiful and the ugly, the successes and the failures. Nothing is hidden from him, and yet he pursues a relationship with us. What an awesome concept! Our Lord is there to celebrate our most meager victories, yet he is not repelled by our most despicable failures. That is the friendship Jesus offers us: faithful, perfect, never-failing.

Not only is Jesus our friend, he is also our healer. In Isaiah 53:5, we read:

But he was pierced for our transgressions, he was crushed for our iniquities; the punishment that brought us peace was upon him, and by his wounds we are healed.

Christ's healing comes in three distinct ways. First and foremost, he *heals us from our sin-sickness.* This is the eternal healing we talked about in chapter 8, the healing that cements our firm foundation in place.

Second, *Christ heals our physical bodies.* Even though this is what most people think of when we say "healing," it is probably the least important of the three. Surely it is scriptural to pray for the healing hand of God, yet we also know that our physical bodies are temporal. In the midst of great illness, it is hard to add "if it's your will" to our prayers. But we must rest assured that in his perfect timing, and in his perfect way, God is totally capable of healing our every illness.

Third, *Christ heals us emotionally.* Craig knows all about this type of healing. Since his early teenage years, he had struggled with sexual identity issues. He has been involved in one relationship after another, both bisexual and homosexual.

At the age of six, Craig was sexually abused by an older neighborhood boy. Years of counseling and therapy assured him this issue had been dealt with.

At a retreat, Craig surprised everyone by stating, "I can't ask God to heal me. I'm too ashamed."

"Show us how you feel toward God," someone suggested.

Craig thought for a minute, then he sat down in the middle of the floor. Pulling his knees up to his chest, he held them tightly with this arms, and tucked his head down as far as it would go. "This is how I feel," he said. "Like a naughty six-year-old."

"We see where you are," another person said, "but where is God?"

"He isn't anywhere around me," Craig answered. "God is holy and I am bad."

A minister who was with us spoke up. "Let me play the part of Jesus, Craig." He got up from his chair and went to sit on the floor beside Craig. He pulled his knees up to his chest and held them tightly with his arms. Not a word was spoken as the two men sat in silence.

"This is what Jesus does, Craig," the minister finally said. "He stays right beside you through your pain."

You may be one of the many who has battled depression or job burn-out or prolonged stress. You may have suffered from physical, sexual, or emotional abuse. You may have been raised by an alcoholic parent, or perhaps you were emotionally abandoned as a child. Perhaps in your pain, you, like Craig, have decided that God just isn't in your picture at all.

Regardless of how you feel, God the healer is right there beside you. Jesus the Christ, the Son of the living God, is your most faithful friend and your most powerful healer.

BE TRULY FREE

We have identified the barriers between our heads and our hearts. We have examined the deceptions that beset us and have seen them for what they are. We have made sure that the foundation on which we are building is firm and secure. Then we have gone about dismantling the barriers that block our head knowledge from our heart experience. Now we are beginning to know what it is to be truly free.

But let us add one last word. More than any other thing, we see people longing to reduce Life to a predictable equation. The most common question is, "Why?" We understand that question. We have asked it ourselves. We, too, have longed for the safety and control that a forthright equation would offer.

Good news! We *have* a predictable equation. God gave it to us in his Word. His word is true and eternal. Between the covers of the Bible are all the necessary ingredients for a barrier-free life in relationship with the Almighty God. We read about a God who is always faithful, who never changes, yet who is infinitely creative in the ways he chooses to relate to us.

In the Bible, we discover that the shortest line between our heads and our hearts goes directly through the God of the universe.

Questions for Reflection and Discussion

1. Set aside some quiet time. Ask God to speak to you through Scripture. Ask him to give you one or two key Scriptures to stand on during this process. Write these down on note cards and leave them in places that you can easily spot them. The journey will not always be easy, and

you will need his encouragement along the way—and there is nothing more powerful than his Word!

2. Create a "victory list," reminding yourself of the times when you know God has been faithful. Put this on your mirror or by a bedside table. Use this as extra encouragement for the difficult times.

BREAKING THROUGH TO THE HEART

We hope this book has helped you understand the types of barriers and deceptions which keep you from having a heart knowledge of God. However, simply understanding the concepts and ideas in this book is not enough. This section offers you a way to "dig" deeper.

Most of us are not aware of the level of the barriers in our lives, nor of the essential concepts those barriers block. The following lists of symptoms and tests were designed to help you determine which specific areas, terms, and words may be blocking the lifeline between your head and heart. Each specific category begins with a symptoms check followed by a test called "A Checkup from the Heart Up."

We have also included a variety of creative exercises and activities which are designed to help you begin the breakthrough process. We have used all of these at our retreats and conferences and they have proved very helpful. Even though they were originally designed for use in groups, they can be just as effective for individual use.

1
HOLINESS, SIN

Symptoms: Read the statements under each of the next four sections and check off the ones you feel apply to you. Once you have finished all four sections, add up the check marks in each section and write the total in the spaces provided.

Behavioral

✓ You find yourself striving to be "good enough" to earn Christ's love and acceptance. Conditional love may be something that is very familiar to you.

____ You are aware of extremes in behavior: drivenness and overactivity versus lack of direction and passivity.

✓ Super-responsible or super-irresponsible are words which describe you.

____ Sometimes you become weary of the effort it takes to please God and you feel like giving up.

____ You find yourself surrounded by rules to live by as a Christian. As you obey these rules, you run the risk of depending upon them rather than God.

✓ **Total of Behavioral Section**

Psychological/Emotional

✓ If you can identify with the need to be right, you may be spending quite a bit of time rehearsing things that have gone wrong. Situations are played out, over and over again until you find the right solution, *if* you find the right solution. This process may wear you out.

✓ Guilt and shame are pervasive emotions. You may wonder if you will ever be able to truly leave the past behind, or make the changes you want to make.

___ You use questions such as, "What difference does it make really? Why bother?"

✓ Depression, hopelessness, and apathy may accompany your inability to make the changes you want to make.

✓ Rest, joy, and peace are fairly foreign emotions.

4 **Total of Psychological/Emotional Section**

Relational

✓ Tasks and projects often feel more comfortable to you than relating to people.

✓ Control is a powerful word for you. Staying in control means that you can be "good" enough. Losing control means that you are vulnerable to sin and failure. This leaves you trusting in yourself far more than anyone else, including God.

✓ The need to be in control may keep you from enjoying close relationships because people complain that your "rules" or expectations are just too stressful.

✓ Loneliness may drive you to unhealthy relationships where you often end up in the "savior" role. But, you may find yourself "crucified" in these relationships on a regular basis.

4 **Total of Relational Section**

Spiritual

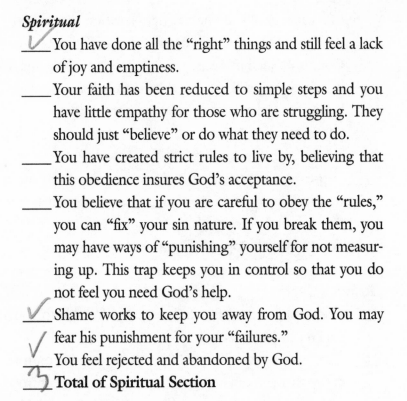

____ You have done all the "right" things and still feel a lack of joy and emptiness.

____ Your faith has been reduced to simple steps and you have little empathy for those who are struggling. They should just "believe" or do what they need to do.

____ You have created strict rules to live by, believing that this obedience insures God's acceptance.

____ You believe that if you are careful to obey the "rules," you can "fix" your sin nature. If you break them, you may have ways of "punishing" yourself for not measuring up. This trap keeps you in control so that you do not feel you need God's help.

____ Shame works to keep you away from God. You may fear his punishment for your "failures."

____ You feel rejected and abandoned by God.

____ **Total of Spiritual Section**

Did you score higher in one section than the others? If so, this could indicate that you have a problem in this area. You are encouraged to take this information before God in prayer.

Checkup from the Heart Up: Read each of the following statements, choosing the term that best describes your response. Put the number above the term in the blank beside each statement.

1	2	3	4	5	6	7
ALWAYS	VERY OFTEN	OFTEN	SOMETIMES	SELDOM	VERY SELDOM	NEVE

_1_ 1. I tend to have high expectations of myself and others.

_4_ 2. I have difficulty giving myself permission to relax and just have fun.

_2_ 3. I am aware of a lack of joy in my life.

_2_ 4. When mistakes are made, I can easily become critical of myself or others.

_4_ 5. I find it hard work to be a "good" Christian.

_3_ 6. I struggle with the idea of God being the ultimate authority in my life.

_3_ 7. If I am really a "new creation," I wonder how I can continue to do some of the things I do.

_2_ 8. I wonder how God could really love me.

_3_ 9. When I do something wrong, I feel condemned and unworthy of love.

_3_ 10. I have difficulty trusting those in authority over me.

_28_ Total. Use the scale below to interpret your scores.

Scoring:

50 - 70

You have probably wrestled with these words and have come to terms with the sovereignty and mystery of God in a way that leaves you open to learn more about him, but also leaves you at peace.

35 - 50

You are aware of difficulties in these areas, but you may not have related them to a spiritual struggle.

0 - 35

You are struggling with barriers which are greatly affecting your life. They will not go away by themselves. It is up to you to begin to take definitive action and ask for God's help to bring them down.

EXERCISES AND ACTIVITIES

Activity: Consuming Fire

Goal: An exercise for groups to understand the concept of God's holiness.

Time Needed: 1 hour

Materials Needed:

poster paper, at least one large sheet per small group

multi-colored construction paper packs, one per group

colored markers, wide—two packs per group

scissors and glue, tape- 2 each per group

other creative "bits", like aluminum foil, interesting props, etc.

Instructions:

1. Spend some time in your small group "brainstorming." Take about ten minutes and talk about the word Holy. Choose someone to be secretary and have that person record the key words you come up with.

2. Next, try to think of symbols associated with the words you have chosen.

3. From these symbols, try to create a three-dimensional work of art or even a "living picture" or charade. The group can agree on one idea, or have a variety of ideas. Remember to get in touch with the things of the heart— not just what you know is truth in your head. Allow about fifteen minutes for creative time.

5. Each group will then present its work, allowing about five minutes maximum time per presentation. They simply make it available for all to see, or create their living picture. Have the other groups guess what they have tried to portray, then the presenting group can share what they were attempting.

6. The leader or facilitator should sum up what has been presented. Be prepared for God to surprise you with the creative things that show up—planned and unplanned! Close in prayer.

A Personal Exercise

Go back through the symptoms that you have checked in this section. On a separate piece of paper, write down what believing this statement would say to you about God's character, his love, and your identity in him. Once you have written these things down, make them a matter of prayer, asking God to reveal his truth. Give him "permission" to begin to break through the barriers that exist and touch your heart in a new way!

A Deeper Look

Ask God to help you find a symbol that represents the barriers you have identified. Journal what this means to you. Next, spend some time in prayer as you meditate on the significance of this symbol. Ask God to speak to you through it, telling you what he wants you to know about yourself and him. See if you can find any scriptural references to this symbol. Write down the verses that are applicable and ask God to speak to you through them.

2
GRACE, JUSTIFICATION, AND FORGIVENESS

Symptoms: Read the statements under each of the next four sections and check off the ones you feel apply to you. Once you have finished all four sections, add up the check marks in each section and write the total in the spaces provided.

Behavioral

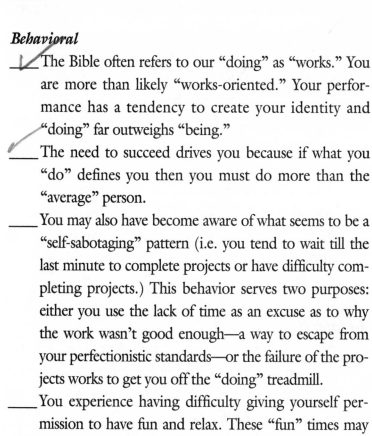

____The Bible often refers to our "doing" as "works." You are more than likely "works-oriented." Your performance has a tendency to create your identity and "doing" far outweighs "being."

____The need to succeed drives you because if what you "do" defines you then you must do more than the "average" person.

____You may also have become aware of what seems to be a "self-sabotaging" pattern (i.e. you tend to wait till the last minute to complete projects or have difficulty completing projects.) This behavior serves two purposes: either you use the lack of time as an excuse as to why the work wasn't good enough—a way to escape from your perfectionistic standards—or the failure of the projects works to get you off the "doing" treadmill.

____You experience having difficulty giving yourself permission to have fun and relax. These "fun" times may cause you to feel guilty for not being productive.

_____ When a mistake is made, you must find the person or thing to blame. Someone or something must pay.

__✓__ You don't like to admit you are wrong or have made a mistake—to you, failure is not acceptable.

__3__ **Total of Behavioral Section**

Psychological/Emotional

__✓__ You have a number of rules for living that begin with expressions like, "I should," "I ought to," "I have to," "I must."

_____ You feel guilty for much of what happens around you. Somehow, you "should" have done something or you "could" have done something in the situation.

__✓__ A predictable and fair system for life is important to you, and having such a system makes you feel in control.

__✓__ There may also be a sense of abandonment and a question which recurs: "Why do I have to work so hard to be seen and noticed? Can anyone love me just for me?"

__3__ **Total of Psychological/Emotional Section**

Relational

__✓__ "Love" is a word you question. More than likely the love you have experienced and even given to others has been conditional. It is based around performance and is learned through messages like, "I will love you if… you are good…, you are successful…, you look acceptable," and so on.

✓ You have felt used by others in relationships. Perhaps people have accused you of using them.

____ You know what it means to be caught in the trap of comparing yourself to others.

✓ Being "special" is important to you and it may drive you in your relationships.

✓ You find it much easier to give than receive. The idea of owing anyone does not sit well with you.

✓ **Total of Relational Section**

Spiritual

____ Three key questions may plague you. While these may not be voiced to others, you hear them inside. "Can I trust God's love for me? What does his love really mean? Do I have security in my relationship with him?"

____ If we could hear your secret thoughts, we might hear you questioning whether you are really saved.

____ **Total of Spiritual Section**

Did you score higher in one section than the others? If so, this could indicate that you have a problem in this area. You are encouraged to take this information before God in prayer.

Checkup from the Heart Up: Read each of the following statements, choosing the term that best describes your response. Put the number above the term in the blank beside each statement.

1	2	3	4	5	6	7
ALWAYS	VERY OFTEN	OFTEN	SOMETIMES	SELDOM	VERY SELDOM	NEVER

_____ 1. My "self-talk" is made up of many expressions like "I should," "I ought to," "I have to," etc.

_____ 2. Whenever something goes wrong around me, I somehow feel responsible for what happened.

_____ 3. I have difficulty trusting God.

_____ 4. I find myself in many situations where I will have to do something myself in order to have it done right.

_____ 5. It is important that things are "fair."

_____ 6. I have difficulty forgiving myself when I make a mistake.

_____ 7. It is easy to hold a grudge when someone hurts me or does something wrong.

_____ 8. I do not like to owe anyone.

_____ 9. I question if God truly forgives me.

_____ 10. If something goes wrong, I am compelled to figure out what happened, make it right, or know whom to blame.

_____ **Total. Use the scale below to interpret your scores.**

50 - 70

You have probably wrestled with these words and have come to terms with the sovereignty and mystery of God in a way that leaves you open to learn more about him, but also leaves you at peace.

35 - 50

You are aware of difficulties in these areas, but you may not have related them to a spiritual struggle.

0 - 35

You are struggling with barriers in this area which are greatly affecting your life. They will not go away by themselves. It is up to you to begin to take definitive action and ask for God's help to bring them down.

Exercises and Activities

Activity: The Unforgiveness Bus

Goal: To help people see the burden of carrying around so many people, places and things that are with us because of unforgiveness.

Time: 30 minutes

Instructions:

1. Divide into groups with six to eight people per group. Have each group create a picture of what would be in this "bus" and what the journey would be like. Each group will need to choose a "driver" who is carrying the load and can use words to describe what they pick up along the way. Choose one group to focus on bringing their load to Christ, what they would do, what Christ would do, and what life would be like without the "load."

2. Allow ten minutes for brainstorming the assigned "pictures."

3. Each group should find a "private" place to create and practice its presentation. Allow as much as thirty minutes, if needed, for the creative time. The use of props is encouraged.

4. Present the picture to the group. Allow no more than two minutes per picture.

5. The group facilitator can generate discussion following each presentation. Be sure to draw out why we keep traveling like this, what we hope to accomplish, and what this says about our relationship with God and others. What barriers prevent us from unloading the "passengers" and baggage to Christ?

6. Close with prayer, inviting each participant to be challenged in a new way to accept God's grace and his forgiveness.

A Personal Exercise

Try to remember times when you have received grace (unmerited favor) from someone or from God. Write these down. Now think about the word "justification." Test the "grace" list you have just written. Go back and see what you did in each case to "deserve" the gift of grace you received. Was it true grace, or was it conditional? What messages have these experiences taught you about grace and love? What barriers may have been created as a result of these?

It is also possible that you may struggle to remember any "grace encounters." What does this say to you? What kind of barriers would this create?

If you have discovered true experiences with grace, what do these teach you about giving and receiving love? How do they help you begin to understand the true meaning of forgiveness?

A Deeper Look

Once again you may want to look back at the symptoms you have checked or the test statements that scored a low value. Make a list of these and try to place them in one of the barrier categories: language, experience, distorted belief, emotional defense, control. Use this list to help you see the area of greatest struggle.

Take another sheet of paper and entitle it "Misperceptions of God." Use the statements you have been working with and ask yourself what believing these say about God's character. Write down your thoughts. You will probably struggle at this point, because you know these are "wrong" thoughts and will try to talk yourself out of putting them down on paper. But, do it anyway. This exercise helps to bring the lies out into the light. This list can now become your prayer "list."

Ask God to help you begin to trust him to show you who he really is. Give him permission to begin to break through the barriers. Ask him to bring his Word to you in a new way, a way that will counter your misperceptions with new revelation of his character and love for you.

Once again you may want to find something that symbolically represents the new truths God has shown you. Do a Bible study on the scriptural significance of this symbol. Let this symbol be a concrete reminder of the special breakthrough the Lord has brought to your heart.

3
OBEDIENCE, REGENERATION, AND PEACE

Symptoms: Read the statements under each of the next four sections and check off the ones you feel apply to you. Once you have finished all four sections, add up the check marks in each section and write the total in the spaces provided.

Behavioral

____ You stay extremely busy to avoid thinking or feeling too much about personal matters.

____ Loyalty and steadfastness are words that friends use to describe you.

____ You struggle with setting personal boundaries because you desire other people's approval.

____ You are known as a "super-nice" person.

____ You are known as a rebel and struggle with authority issues.

____ **Total of Behaviorial Section**

Psychological/Emotional

____ There is always a sense of something about to go wrong, or that things are not quite right. This creates a backdrop of anxiety and a need to control people and things.

_____ You struggle with low self esteem. It seems that others are more important than you. You just do not feel "special."

_____ Love just hasn't worked out well for you and you wonder why.

_____ You tend to disassociate or "numb" yourself when you face difficult situations. You can easily "check out" when too much is going on.

_____ Abandonment and rejection issues, guilt and shame are very strong in your life.

5 **Total of Psychological/Emotional Section**

Relational

_____ You feel like a "doormat" in relationships. You have difficulty saying no.

_____ People expect you to "do" for them, but it sometimes seems hard to get anyone to "hear" your needs.

_____ Your relationships tend to be either non-confrontive and passive, or the opposite—conflict is pervasive.

_____ Your need for peace causes you to give in to things that really matter to you.

4 **Total of Relational Section**

Spiritual

_____ You believe that "doing" for God means you are accepted and approved.

____ You wonder if you really matter to God and that leaves you feeling anxious and fearful.

____ Personal areas of struggle leave you feeling shamed, condemned, and unaccepted by God.

____ The hopelessness and powerlessness you may feel often leave you questioning God's power and faithfulness. You wonder: Is God really big enough for what I face? Has he truly made me into a "new creation" or is that just some nice idea?

____ You find yourself in a constant war to stay committed to God.

____ **Total of Spiritual Section**

Did you score higher in one section than the others? If so, this could indicate that you have a problem in this area. You are encouraged to take this information before God in prayer.

Checkup from the Heart Up: Read each of the following statements, choosing the term which best describes your response. Put the number above the term in the blank beside each statement.

1	2	3	4	5	6	7
ALWAYS	VERY OFTEN	OFTEN	SOMETIMES	SELDOM	VERY SELDOM	NEVER

_2_ 1. I become depressed when I fail.

_4_ 2. I have unexplained anxiety.

_4_ 3. I find it difficult to relax or rest, if things are not in order.

_4_ 4. People tell me I worry too much.

_1_ 5. I have difficulty praying and knowing God's will for my life.

_2_ 6. There are certain aspects about my character that I want to change, but I do not believe I could ever successfully do so.

_2_ 7. I become depressed when someone criticizes me or points out a mistake I have made.

_4_ 8. I fear what God might do to me.

_3_ 9. I am compelled to tell others the "correct" way when I see them doing something wrong.

_2_ 10. I feel that certain experiences have basically ruined my life.

_28_ **Total. Use the scale below to interpret your scores.**

50 - 70

You have probably wrestled with these words and have come to terms with the sovereignty and mystery of God in a way that leaves you open to learn more about him, but also leaves you at peace.

35 - 50

You are aware of difficulties in these areas, but you may not have related them to a spiritual struggle.

0 - 35

You are struggling with barriers which are greatly affecting your life. They will not go away by themselves. It is up to you to begin to take definitive action and ask for God's help to bring them down.

Exercises and Activities
Activity: Building Barriers

Goal: An exercise for groups to understand how barriers are built in the areas of obedience, regeneration and peace.

Time Needed: 1 to 1½ hours

Materials Needed:

poster paper, at least one large sheet per small group

multi-colored construction paper packs, one per group

wide colored markers, two packs per group

scissors, glue, and tape—two each per group

other creative "bits" such as aluminum foil, interesting props, etc.

Instructions:

1. Divide into at least three groups of six to eight people per group. Each group should be assigned one of the words obedience, regeneration, and peace, or they may want to choose the word they work with.

2. Allow ten minutes for "brainstorming" where members think of various types of barriers that could be built from this word—barriers which keep us from experiencing God in our hearts. Choose someone to be "secretary" to record key words and ideas.

3. Next, try to think of symbols associated with the words you have chosen.

4. From these symbols, build a three-dimensional picture of the "wall," the "barrier." The group can agree on one idea, or have a variety of ideas represented in its presentation. Reminder: get in touch with the things of the heart-not just what you know is truth in your heads. Allow about thirty minutes creation time.

5. Each group will then present its work, allowing about five minutes maximum time per presentation.

6. After all the presentations are finished, ask for a volunteer who will come to the front and help the group see how effective these barriers can be:

   a. When the individual is in place (in front of the group) have him or her sit in the floor. Next, ask each group to come and put their picture of barriers around this person.

   b. Allow this example to generate discussion. How will this barrier interfere with how this person is able to relate to others? What kinds of problems will it create? How will this barrier affect this person's self-esteem and identity in Christ? How will this barrier affect the individual's relationship with God?

7. The facilitator should close this exercise by asking everyone to think about what barriers might be around them and what they would want to do about them. Close in prayer, asking God to bring fresh revelation and his loving touch to these wounded places.

A Personal Exercise

Choose one word (obedience, regeneration or peace) that you would most like to work with. You will need three sheets of loose-leaf paper. Each should have one of the following headings: Me, Others, God. If you choose the word obedience, start with the Me page and ask God to help you remember situations where you experienced "obedience." What happened? What messages did you receive? Go through each page like this. When you finish, look back at the five categories of barriers: language, experience, distorted beliefs, emotional defenses, and control. Try to put what you have written into the appropriate categories. What does this tell you? Write out a prayer asking God to begin the breakthrough process, and be specific about the areas that need his touch.

A Deeper Look

In the exercise above, you worked hard to identify some problem areas. Refer back to chapter 8 and the building stones. In the questions for reflection and discussion at the end of each chapter, you identified key Scriptures for each one. Add these to your journal and see how they apply to the breakthrough you seek with the word you chose. Next, look at chapter 9 and follow the four-step plan for "barrier destruction." Once you have applied this process, you have a model with which to approach other key words of the faith, attributes of God that you struggle with, and so on. This process can give you powerful God-given tools for barrier destruction. The walls need never be built again!

MORE INFORMATION ABOUT RETREATS AND CONFERENCES:

Healing for the Nations is an interdenominational, international, Christ-centered and biblically based ministry that strives to bring healing and wholeness to God's people. Each month regularly scheduled intensive eight-day retreats are held in Colorado Springs, Colorado, at historic Glen Eyrie, the Navigators' International Conference Center. In addition to this location, we have a number of bases around the world which also schedule retreats, conferences and training programs. These include: Kona, Hawaii; Einigen, Switzerland; and Lancaster, England. Participants come from all over the world to meet God in a new and dynamic way. These individuals come to retreats for a variety of reasons. Perhaps they are in a transition place: divorce, change in career, life changes, etc. Others may be struggling with a sense of emptiness within and need a fresh encounter with God. Some come to the retreats because they have not been able to break free of destructive patterns in their thoughts, attitudes, emotions, or behavior.

For more information contact our toll free number.

800-483-2841 *or*

Office: 719-282-0584   Fax: 719-282-1589

MAILING ADDRESSES
Colorado Springs: Healing for the Nations
PO Box 62610
Colorado Springs, Co. 80962-2610

Kona, Hawaii: Healing for the Nations
PO Box 967
Kona, Hawaii 96745